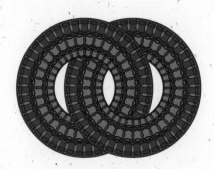

We Aren't
Who
We Are

and this world isn't either

We Aren't
Who
We Are

and this world isn't either

Christine Korfhage

CavanKerry ◊ Press LTD.

CavanKerry Press Ltd.
Fort Lee, New Jersey
www.cavankerrypress.org

Library of Congress Cataloging-in-Publication Data

Korfhage, Christine, 1947–
We aren't who we are and this world isn't either / Christine Korfhage. —
1st ed.
p. cm.
ISBN-13: 978-1-933880-04-4
ISBN-10: 1-933880-04-X
I. Title.

PS3611.O7426W4 2007
811'.6—dc22

2007014227

Cover art by James O'Brien © 2006
Author photograph by C. R. Matty
Cover and book design by Peter Cusack

First Edition 2007
Printed in the United States of America

NEW ✧ VOICES

CavanKerry Press is dedicated to springboarding the careers of previously unpublished poets by bringing to print two to three New Voices annually. Manuscripts are selected from open submission; CavanKerry Press does not conduct competitions or charge reading fees.

CavanKerry Press is grateful for the support it receives from the New Jersey State Council on the Arts.

Acknowledgments

Grateful acknowledgment is made to the editors of the following publications and anthology in which these works or earlier versions of them previously appeared.

Art and Understanding: "Rhyme"
Chiron Review: "J.M.J.," "Freebies," "What Can You Do?"
Connecticut River Review: "International School of the Sacred Heart"
IRIS: "The Fruit Stand"
Mad Poets Review: "Picture Perfect" (as "Lighthouse Point")
Nimrod International Journal: "More Than I Knew"
Paterson Literary Review: "Mom's Ring"
Pearl: "Web Stalker"
Red Rock Review: "Lavender"
Snowy Egret: "The Gift"
The Spoon River Poetry Review: "First Death"
"My Father's Voice," appeared in *The Breath of Parted Lips, Voices from The Robert Frost Place,* Volume II, edited by Sydney Lea (CavanKerry Press, 2004).

†††

I was extremely fortunate to work with Nadell Fishman at the Vermont College Adult Degree Program, with April Bernard, David Lehman, Liz Rosenberg, and Jason Shinder at the Bennington Writing Seminars, and with Molly Peacock privately—to each: my deep gratitude, with special thanks to Nadell for her continuing friendship, to Molly for helping shape this manuscript, and to Liz for her generous Foreword.

Immense thanks also to the many other writers, nonwriters, groups, and organizations that supported me during the making of this book, in particular: Stanley Kunitz for saying, "My struggle is to use the life in order to transcend it, to convert it to legend"; Donald Sheehan and The Frost Place for giving me a place to flourish and feel that I belong; Sydney Lea for taking notice; Terry Blythe, Lance Bodie, Julia Crane, Margaret Gavin, Terry

Gavin, Bob Pearsall, and Susan Pearsall for their sustaining encouragement; the folks at the Laconia Athletic and Swim Club for helping me stay limber despite the long hours I spent sitting at this desk; my publisher, Joan Handler, for helping me find the poems that made this book whole; and Nicole, Rob, and Mia for their love, which is indispensable to my life.

.

Es verdad; pues, reprimamos
esta fiera condición,
esta furia, esta ambición,
por si alguna vez soñamos;
y si haremos, pues estamos
en mundo tan singular,
que el vivir solo es soñar;
y la experiencia me enseña
que el hombre que vive sueña
lo que es hasta dispertar.

He speaks the truth.
We must control this savagery,
this wild ambition, this ferocity
in case we dream again.
For surely we'll dream again
when this world seems so strange a place
that all our life is but a dream,
and what I've seen so far tells me
that any man who lives dreams
what he is until at last he wakes.

—Pedro Calderón de la Barca
(1600–1681)

For my family

Contents

Foreword

The first quality that will strike any reader of Christine Korfhage's book of poems, *We Aren't Who We Are and this world isn't either*, is its courage: fierce, intelligent courage in the face of pain, in the midst of family trauma, in the teeth of a lost love, in the trials of being human at all. Simply to live is an act of courage, in its muddled complexity and beauty. Korfhage acknowledges that complexity and raises it up to the level of art.

Contradiction is built into the title of this book. So too is the question of being. Korfhage's work admits no easy answers. "Do I contradict myself? Very well then I contradict myself." Whitman showed us what a glorious mess it is to be human, and Korfhage extends the journey, forging her own path, delicately stepping or marching as she goes. Her poetry is quirky, colloquial, feminine, as many eyed as the fly on the wall. *We Aren't Who We Are* is as fast-paced and dramatic as any novel. Korfhage divides it not into seven parts but seven "chapters." It tells the story of a life. How wonderful it is that she sounds like no one else!

> How old were we? I was fifteen. He, sixteen.
> Or, maybe a bit younger, since I would
> have been wearing my bracelet—the little
> gold ID bracelet he gave me that birthday,
> with *Christine* engraved on the flat surface,
> *Love, Paqui* on the side against my skin.
> We were inside the American Military Cemetery
> standing amid acres of manicured lawns,
> and row upon row of white wooden crosses
> and six-pointed stars, at the center
> of a copse of exotic plants and trees
> behind a stand of flowering pink hibiscus.
> We were kissing.

The poet stands in the center of a copse of "exotic plants and trees," this kiss stands at the center of the universe. Each instant is given its rightful weight. Korfhage's poetry is unadorned, or, certainly, no more adorned than life itself with its "white wooden crosses and six-pointed stars," its "flowering pink hibiscus" and kisses. Who could stop reading here? In fact, who in their right mind would stop reading anytime before the poet lets us go? She will send us off with a poem that ends with a birth and a question, an epilogue that sends us spinning back around to the beginning poem, about the poet's own conception. *We Aren't Who We Are* is unabashedly autobiographical. Precisely because of this, its unapologetic commitment to authenticity, it reaches beyond a particular character, a particular story. Look how lovingly the poet talks about a man met on a plane, a man who turns out to have a haunting story of his own. Everything, everyone has their own story—flowers, neighbors, family, boats, and bells—all of the stories interconnect, flee one another, fall apart and reconvene. Nothing is too small to be beneath her notice—"what about this dragonfly? It, too, / must be remembered. This swarm of gnats. / That canoe someone abandoned on shore. / The marsh grass growing through its missing bottom."

"Speaking truth" is thrown down like a gauntlet in the opening quote from the Spanish poet and playwright Pedro Calderón de la Barca. There is never an instant in this collection of poems when one feels the poet telling us anything less than the truth, insofar as she can gather it in her arms, like one trying to carry water without a pail. *We Aren't Who We Are* is multivoiced; scraps of conversation flow murmuring through it. One poem records "Mom's Last Notes to Me and Herself": *"DON'T SELL THE HOUSE / IT'S MY ACE IN THE HOLE . . . Don't talk using up air."* Korfhage is never just using up air. Her language is deliberately colloquial, like the marvelous poets Marie Howe and Sharon Olds. It is elegant and achingly honest, like her teacher / poet Jason Shinder. But she is always forging her own way. At times when the sadness seems almost unbearable, she will suddenly erupt in humor, a comic pratfall, or manic leap, as at the end of "Facing the Mirror" when the middle-aged poet in aerobics class catches herself "thinking / about that man I try not to think about— / the one who's so much younger than me— / the one who just yesterday referred to / my daughter's new dog as *your grandpuppy*, / I flew up on my step, and moved/through that routine like a woman possessed."

In the final chapter of this book, Korfhage moves more explicitly into the kind of searching one would expect from a passionate seeker. Haven't all of the autobiographical details amounted to a kind of modern-day Confessions of St. Augustine? Here too there is stolen fruit, "all five of us cousins, sunburned, / lips stained from eating into the profits," here too a desire for wealth, prestige, safety, security, and a thirsting for deeper meaning. "Each Sunday for the past twenty years," she writes in the Zen-simple poem "The Bell," "I've walked through the woods / to a small satsang hall to hear the words / of wise men, mystics and saints." Now, in the body of this poem, "... for the first time in many years, / I did not go to the hall. I stayed home / writing and rewriting the words of this poem. / I lost track of time. / Then I heard the bell." The poem itself is full of a gentle ringing—"hall" and "bell"; "time", "home", "poem", "time." Perhaps the most ambitious poem in the book comes also toward the end, "What If?" In it, the poet is "meditating on my heredity." She is remembering "good / simple people of faith who went to Mass / every Sunday and never spoke ill of anyone," and her own "younger self," her pilgrimages. As the poet writes she begins to doubt, to descend into a dark night of the soul in which "there is no other side—if all / that exists is this one life." The poet imagines that a fish nibbles her bones after her death; is caught by a child; fried in a large iron skillet and is set out "on a warm platter" for the family to eat, "with the evening sun coming through / the screens."

Here is the essential moment then, the moment of being and non-being:

> What if this is what becomes of me after death?
> What if this is all? If this is it?
> How could I consider myself cheated?
> How could I not count myself blessed?

This is no ordinary poet, no ordinary book of poems. Equally passionate about life —"Him. Him. Him. His smell. / He always smelled of lavender" —and death —"*If I die first will you come to my funeral? / Absolutely. I'll be there.*" Korfhage is a poet worth listening to, a bird singing from a bare branch, beautifully.

Liz Rosenberg,
2007

We Aren't
Who
We Are

and this world isn't either

More Than I Knew

That night in Tio Juan's—my fifty-third birthday—
when with our second margarita
we took turns predicting each other's futures,
and I said in five years he'd be married
with a baby, and he said, *why not two?*
so I said, *with who?*
and in that voice that means he's slightly drunk,
he said, *the town 'ho*—
and then, when it was his turn—I swear
he sounded sad—and he said I'd *still* be
eighteen years older than him,
then fell into silence,
I knew . . . I knew what I always knew: no matter
how much older he seemed—even fatherly—
oh, I knew the impossibility.

I knew it pouring my tea, digging
in the garden, cooking, falling asleep.
I knew it that Christmas Eve I spent
at his house, when he played our favorite CD—
the one with "Brutha Iz" singing
"Somewhere Over the Rainbow,"
and we ate his special pasta with shrimp and parsley,
then drove through the snow
to midnight Mass, and when he pushed
that heavy wooden door open, and oh,
it was lovely—the choir singing in French,
the whole place done up in red—
and when he whispered into my ear,
I picked the church, now you pick the pew.

3

I knew it at my daughter's wedding,
when it was hard to know: when I swear
he looked jealous watching me dance
with that handsome Greek with the long last name;
and when it was easy to know:
when I was carrying my niece's new baby
high up on my shoulder and he came over
and said, *Just think, you could be a grandma soon!*
I even knew it that morning last spring
when we drove three hours through a rainstorm
to see the inn we'd win if we won that essay
contest he said we should enter;
but after we spent how many weeks
writing how many drafts that *implied*
we were married, *suggested*
we were married, said without *saying*,
we were married?—I lost my bearings.

Which is why that hot day last August we spent
on his boat, when we finally pulled back up
to the dock, and he climbed out to fix the lines,
and I stayed on board gathering our things,
and his chest—those blond white hairs I loved
to look at that reminded me of my father's—
came so close to my face, if I just lifted
my head a little I could have kissed them—
I didn't want to hear he'd run into someone
from college—no, not *someone*—an old love,
who'd married, moved, divorced, moved back.
I didn't want to know she was staying
in a nearby cabin, he'd probably drop in.
I didn't want to see his nipples harden,
those little darts of lust shoot out of him.
And just as I was feeling their sting,
I didn't want life to play one of its brutal tricks,

when in his forgivable ignorance,
he stopped what he was doing, looked down,
and said her name, *Louise, nice don't you think?*
But I did well. I didn't keel over
or jump in the lake and not come up.
I didn't throw my hands over my ears
and shriek, *Please don't do this to me.*
I acted normal, nodded my head, said,
Yes. Kind of old-fashioned.

Not until I was alone did I let
the wild terror out. Louise, my mother's name.
Louise, my father's bride.
Poor, mad Louise, who wore sexy dresses
and dragged me with her to nightspots
where she carried on with God knows
how many men, while I learned to drink
grasshoppers growing up. Louise, who blew
smoke in my face and called me cunt,
whom I begged my father to leave—oh, why
did he stay? Louise, whom I loved and hated,
and watched—no, *wanted* to die—whose ashes
I tossed in the sea, as far from my father's
as I possibly could.
Oh, why did she have to come back?

Later, sleepless, exhausted, I kept seeing
the glimpse I'd caught of him on the dock—
the animal, the bristling, the want.
And giving in to it, as I reached down
and made love to myself, the image of him
touching her, loving her, kept slipping into
my head, till I felt myself becoming her,
was her. And he was on top of me,
eye to eye, nipple to nipple, sex to sex.

And when he took that part of himself unknown to me,
and plunged it deep into my body, I swear I *felt* it.
I swear I saw him soaring into pleasure.
And as I came to the end with him, I swear
I heard his broken sigh, *oh, Louise.*
I swear it. I swear on this mahogany
bed that holds the ghosts of my makers,
this marriage bed on which I was conceived.

Chapter One

First Confession

Sister Dolora said the words.
We repeated them.
She said them again. Slowly.
Hunched over our desks,
we squeezed freshly sharpened pencils
till they dented our fingers, carefully
printing every word to be memorized.
The next day Sister announced,
Christine Korfhage will be the first to recite.
I stood up straight, shiny religious medals
dangling from my smooth chest. *Oh my God,*
I am partly sorry for having offended Thee . . .
Red-faced, Sister blessed herself twice.
No. No. No.
Heart-i-ly sorry. Repeat after me.
So I did.
But I knew I was telling a lie.
And I knew God knew it, too.

White

I don't remember the rooming house
my parents bought after Dad came home
from the war, or the day he climbed to the roof,
and while cleaning leaves from the gutter,
fell. I don't remember mornings Mom got up
before dawn and cooked for nine men,
or any of the chores she finished by noon—
backbreaking work which before the accident
took her and Dad all day. I don't remember
afternoons she dressed me in a little
red snowsuit, then took me by the hand
as we walked down the steep front steps
and crossed the street to Aunt Dee's. In fact,
I don't remember Aunt Dee, who watched me
while Mom caught the downtown bus
to Pearl Street, and ran Karmani's switchboard
trying to make ends meet
since Dad could no longer moonlight
driving drunks home in a cab.

I just remember Mom, a wreck. A pill-
popping neurotic, who, when not throwing
a fit, or weeping—rocking back and forth,
murmuring, *nobody loves me*,
to that hideous stuffed mouse dressed
in an apron and scullery cap she bought
at a crafts fair and liked to hold on her lap—
sat at the kitchen table drinking Sanka,
smoking Kents, and telling me this story
so many times, I could almost see Dad falling,
almost taste the eggs she cooked each morning,

almost smell the Spic 'N Span.
Don't you remember? she'd say,
I always picked you up by nine,
I never skipped your bath.
You must remember SOMETHING.
And I'd say, *Mom, how could I?*
I was just a baby—a year and a half,
then say I needed to be somewhere.

Sometimes though, out of guilt, or pity,
or perhaps love, I'd stay. If she said,
Chrissy, give me a hug,
I did, holding my breath so as not to breathe
the smoke, hoping it wouldn't last long.
Otherwise, I'd just sit there across the table—
close, but not too close to this woman
I found so hard to bear: my mother,
whom everyone called *the biggest mistake*
your father ever made.
And sometimes while looking at her,
my mind would drift,
and I'd recall someone—Aunt Dee?—
carrying me into a room,
putting me down.
White. I'd remember white.
White floor. White walls.
A lady. White dress. White shoes. A nurse?
I'd remember a bed. White sheets.
A tunnel of plaster.
I'd see my father's arm, as white
as this paper, sticking out
a hole in the plaster.
And as I watched him reach
under his pillow,
Mom would fade, then be gone altogether—

and I'd see the smile on my father's face
as he watched me walk
toward the licorice stick he held
in his outstretched hand.

Albany and Valatie, New York
1951–1954

When I was four, my brother was born.
My mother gave him a bottle,
sang *Too-Ra-Loo-Ra-Loo-Ra*,
and gazed into his eyes.
When my father came home
he gave me a bag of M&M's.
I took them to my room.
One by one I shoved them
up each nostril, till I felt one
near the corner of my eye.
I called for my father.
Listened for his footsteps.
He didn't get angry.
He got a pair of blunt-tipped tweezers,
and sat me on his lap.
He shone a bright light on me.
It was warm.
He said, *Tilt your head back.*
Then his face close to mine,
those blue eyes looking up my nose,
he removed a whole red one . . .
a chocolate-covered shard of yellow . . .
more yellow...a sliver of green . . .

*

I'm scared, I said, as Dad tucked me in
that first night in our new home.
Of what?
Robbers.

Oh, them, he said. *They'll never bother us.*
How come?
We live in the nicest house on the block.
Anyone can see we've used up all our money.
Oh, yeah, I said, relieved.

*

I woke in the middle of the night,
called for my father,
climbed out of bed to look for him.
He was standing in the kitchen,
his hands resting on the back
of Mom's chair. She sat there
stiff as a mannequin, her eyes
fixed on the wall. It seemed
more yellow than before. Bright
like the sun, or a buttercup.
What's wrong with Mommy?
Nothing. Go back to sleep.
In bed, I lay myself belly-down.
Tucked my arm under the pillow.
Drew one knee up to my side.
But when I closed my eyes,
I saw her sitting in that chair,
staring at the wall.

*

Around and around we went,
then we raced past the barn,
across the yard, and into the house
where our mother was born.
Grandpa yelled, *Get those god-*
damned kids out of here!

13

Gram tried, *Kids, outside!*
Rich ducked under the table,
ran for the stairs.
Inside the stairwell,
three steps ahead,
he reached the landing,
pulled down his pants,
spun around. He was holding
his penis, s t r e t c h i n g it out.
I thought, *Maybe it's a finger.*
Then I heard him shout,
One more step and I'll squirt!
Not daring to move,
I shut my mouth, stared up
at that nozzle. Saw
for the first time: a man.

First Death

The summer Aunt Pat left Uncle Rob
and moved herself and three small kids
back to the farm, my father took a job
overseas. So Mom, who always did
whatever Pat did, moved herself
and my brother and me back to the farm,
and we lived with Pat and the kids
in the big house close to the road,
unless Mom and Pat were having
one of their fights, then we lived
in the little house next to the fruit stand
with Gram and Grandpa, who had emphysema
and lay under his oxygen tent (except
when he poked his head out to light up
a smoke), and Charlie, the dumb mynah
bird who never talked, squawked, or even
peeped.

But once, after my cousin Dennis and I
finished one of our fights in our secret
swaying green house at the end of the field
—him punching, and me, unable to meet
his strength, trying to inflict some damage
by gouging his eyes out—we raced each other
back through that shoulder-high grass, past
the gnarled trees, the half-collapsed barn
and coops, to the big house hollering,
Who wants to play hide-and-seek?
But no one was there. Or in the fruit stand.
Or the little house. Only Charlie, perched

atop Gramp's empty oxygen tent, hacking
and coughing, and hacking and coughing,
and making the sound the screen door makes
when it slams.

The Fruit Stand

When the last customer drove off
and Gram finally closed up and came in,
lugging baskets of bruised peaches and cherries
for tomorrow's batch of homemade pies,
usually all five of us cousins, sunburned,
lips stained from eating into the profits,
would be kneeling on chairs around the enameled
kitchen table, playing hockey with coins
from her cash box, impatient, waiting for her
to hook a fresh apron over her head,
give us scraps of dough, and a story,
Tell us the one about Grandpa.

Oh, you kids, she'd say. *Again?*
then look out the moth-covered window,
a tendril of honeysuckle dangling
from its upper right corner—too dark now
to see the battered old pickup.
How many mornings had she loaded it,
wedged screaming kids between ladders
and stacks of wooden crates, then started her rounds
up and down the rows of gnarled trees,
before backing up to the rotting platform—
the loading dock where he used to sit
and do nothing but smoke Lucky Strikes?

It was summer, she'd say. *Hot. Like this.*
No . . . worse. I was eighteen, working
at Huyck's Mill, binding wool blankets.
I must have been overcome by the heat.
Morris, somehow he got wind of it . . .

17

Then she'd stop.
And we'd eye each other, loving the pauses,
knowing she'd start leaning into that rolling pin,
her voice, exaggerated, deep, *Louise,*
I don't want to see you working like this.
Marry me. Marry me, Louise, or I'll throw
myself off the Hudson River Bridge.

And we'd be laughing, kneading our little mounds
of dough—conspirators, tilting back on the legs
of those chairs, not understanding completely,
but remembering how much he once scared us:
that one and only tooth—the way it stuck out
over his upper lip, and his voice
whenever he blew up at her,
Get those goddamned kids out of here!

And now, shoulders pulled up to our ears,
we'd clap our sticky mouths, powder them white
with flour dust, a little guilty, perhaps,
but waiting for her to raise her eyes toward—what?
Heaven? The ceiling? That water-stained ceiling?
Her cue for us to join in, *I should've let him jump!*
I should've let him jump!

Airplane

The little boy wearing Hopalong Cassidy
pajamas and cowboy boots,
in the living room with the Oriental rug,
who checks his make-believe watch, says,
Final boarding! then leans his shoulders
into the palms of my upturned hands,
his stomach into the soles of my slipper socks,
is not my brother. He's our father.
And when I press his body up
toward the ceiling and he starts flapping
and flapping his arms, and I carry him
across oceans, and islands, and more oceans,
and continents, we're flying him home.
And sometimes there's turbulence and I wobble
and shake, and sometimes there's strong headwinds,
and sometimes there's thunder and lightning and rain,
and sometimes we run low on gas,
and I lower my legs, cross my arms
over his back, feel his still damp hair
against my cheek, his sheriff's badge digging
into my chest, and we call this refueling,
and then we lift off again, and fly on
and on, and we don't stop—
not when Mom stands in the doorway
as she does every night, saying,
Time for bed, time for bed,
not when she puts her hands on her hips,
bends herself upside down, and says,
I don't want to tell you again!
not even when her face turns red,
and my arms and legs want to give in.

Blue Willow

That Thanksgiving, after all the men
had moved to the living room,
where they were munching peanut brittle
and watching TV, and all the women
had moved to Gram's kitchen
where they were putting away leftovers
and taking turns at the sink, Great-Aunt Stella,
who just pretended to wash so as not to get
her nail polish chipped, handed me
a dinner plate to dry, and said real loud,
*CHRISSY, WHAT DO YOU WANT TO BE
WHEN YOU GROW UP?*
AN ASTRONOMER, I yelled, wiping suds
off that plate's little blue pagoda and tree,
as Mom looked at me funny, and
except for Gram, all the women began clucking
at once. *Boys are the breadwinners. It's their job
to make something of themselves. A girl needs
to find a nice young man to take care of her,
stay home, and raise a family.*
So Great-Aunt Stella, who besides being hard
of hearing, was married to Uncle Ralph
who did nothing his whole life but drink whiskey
and shoot deer, except for the year he contracted
tuberculosis and had a fling with his nurse,
turned to me again. *OH HONEY,
THERE MUST BE A CUTE LITTLE SOMEBODY
YOU HAVE EYES FOR.*
This time, I didn't answer.
I just stood there looking down
at Aunt Stell's high heels, their sides

cut out for bunions.
But later, when I was doing my homework,
I started thinking about Daniel Nolan.
And even though I was at the top
of our class, and he was at the bottom,
I took out a clean sheet of lined paper,
and wrote *Mrs. Daniel Nolan,*
Mrs. Daniel Nolan, until I filled
both sides of the page.

Chapter Two

109 Sherman St.
Albany, New York
March 1, 1957

Dear Christine,

I know I haven't wrote to you before this, But
the letters you wrote have got me going.

Now to get down to busness. Do you know those stamps
you use on your letters. Would you tell me how much
those stamps are. I would like to buy some off you
for my stamp collection.

Oh. And there was two words you spelt wrong
until you put to l's on it and writing you put in too many
t's in it.

Well I jest that's all.

May God bless you.

Your classmate,
Daniel Nolan

Spain
Cartagena, 1997

And when the waiter at the crowded cafe
on Calle Mayor where my father sometimes
took me on Sundays puts a small plate
of olives down on the white tablecloth—
an octagonal dish with *Gran Bar*
printed in green—the same dish I keep soap in
at home—which Dad? Mom? someone
must have swiped from here forty years ago—
I say, *Look, Nicole,* and my daughter
lifts her head from the book she's been reading,
even as we walked all over town looking
for places I once knew: La Escuela
de las Carmelitas, where the nuns tried
in vain to teach me fine stitchery—
closed today, the nuns on retreat;
the train station—now new—but where,
as if yesterday, I could still see Dad, Rich,
Mom and me stepping down onto the dirt
next to the tracks—me, clutching my pocket-
sized Spanish/English dictionary, saying
leche, leche, and Mom, already cranky
from the heat, and soot and all night
swaying back and forth, threatening to
call GE and give them a piece of my mind,
when the man with black fingernails
who reeked of garlic, threw our new Samsonite
into a cart that he hitched to a donkey;
the Hotel Mediterráneo, where we spent
those first nights, and where for the first time
in my eight-year life, I ate clear consommé
and hung clothes in an armoire—

25

where I hoped to stay this time,
but Hotel Mediterráneo isn't a hotel anymore;
and Nicole looks at the dish, nods,
then complains about the heat, again.
Later, driving our rented Fiat
on a two-lane road outside town, I see
a small wooden sign shaped like an arrow
with *Escombreras* written on it, turn east
and follow the high-voltage lines back
past a woman with goats and two men
on bicycles—one with the black ribbon
of mourning tied round his arm—
to the billowing stacks of the power plant
and the rows of white stucco houses winding
their way up the hill behind it and the sea.
Mirror images, it's hard to tell which house
on which row was once ours, but Nicole takes
a picture of me standing in front of one
with blue shutters, then I take one of her.
What can she know of my childhood here?
Of Dad's job? Of afternoons I crawled
between sheets and lay down next to Mom
because Dad—who later, I'd come to know
believed we were all that stood between her
and an institution—asked me to?
Of how Mom reeked of cigarettes and pills—
an acrid odor that caught the back of my throat,
making me retch, making me lie still
as a statue, making me hold my breath?
What can Nicole know of days I ran
down the hill and sat dangling my legs
over the edge of the dock, looking
for the octopus who lived by the pilings,
or played with my little friends, Claude
and Jon Martine, outside their house next door,

always sniffing the dusty air for smells
of cooking—sometimes bread, sometimes what I guessed
was soup, sometimes something else I'll never place—
looking up at their open kitchen window,
hoping to catch sight of their mother
who was French, and like me, named Christine?
What can Nicole know of the day
they came to take my mother away—
how after the ambulance left, I walked
across the narrow driveway and stood
in the unbearable heat? Or the way it felt
when Christine finally looked out
that kitchen window, then disappeared
for a moment before opening the door,
or how I pushed my face into her white apron
and breathed?

Spain
Cartagena, 1955–1956

1.

On the third Sunday of every month
after Mass, my father rang the buzzer
outside that heavy wooden door, promised
Madre Superior I'd be back on time,
then we left those high iron gates.
Sometimes we stopped at Gran Bar,
ordered *un helado de vanilla, una cervesa,*
and if the bulls were in town, we'd join
el paseo along Calle Major as I ran
to catch up with the little boy who sold peanuts:
CACAJUETES! CACAJUETES!
Inside La Plaza de Toros the men would pass
a goatskin sack. Tipping their heads back,
they squirted a long stream of wine
down their throats. My soda was fizzy.
It stung my tongue and ran back out.
Once a young hooligan snuck into the ring.
The bull chased him back and forth,
then he jumped over the barricade.
The bull tried too: *PAUM PAUM*
his hooves pounded the boards. The sound
was like thunder, like a storm you can't see.
The matador was wearing green.
His *traje de luces* was embroidered with sequins.
Back arched, slippers together, he held the cape
low to the ground, gave it a shake, called,
TORO, TORO . . .
and the bull came running as fast as he could.
The cape floated like a ribbon thrown up

in the air, then twirled around them both.
And now the matador, the bull, the cape,
were curling around each other: red, green;
red, black. The crowd was stomping and stomping,
shouting for the bull's festive death.
Sun, sequins, dust—everything was spinning,
spiraling. And I was eight and a half,
wearing that long black braid, black serge uniform,
thick black stockings, standing up on my seat,
arm curled around my father's neck,
sun drunk, happy, hollering.

2.

And on some weekends I came home from school.
If Mom was in bed, not talking, asleep
with her eyes open, Dad would say,
Why don't you lay down with her?
And if it was time for her nerve medicine—
white pills crushed in applesauce—
I'd pinch her nose, and when she opened
her mouth, he'd put the spoon in.
Our house overlooked the jobsite
along the Mediterranean Sea.
When the whistle blew, we'd run
into every room, close wood shutters,
then hurry to the far side and wait
for the blasting to begin—the shower
of dirt, rocks, Mom's hysterics.
At night I loved to stand on the balcony.
Stars sailed on those waters, sometimes
an entire regatta. When Navy ships arrived,
I'd race down the hill, hang around the dock
like the little beggars, all scabs and sores,
who roamed the streets in town. *Hey sailor,*

can you spare a jar of peanut butter?
And if you don't mind, my mother wants
toilet paper—the soft kind.
My father and I were standing on the balcony.
He was wearing his yellow hard hat.
He kept looking down there.
Then he turned his eyes toward me.
They were watery.
Chrissy, he said, *what should we do?*

International School of the Sacred Heart
Tokyo, 1957

Richie's learning Japanese by watching
I Love Lucy *on TV,* Dad writes
on GE stationery from our new home
near Sendai. *Whenever the telephone rings*
he runs to answer, "mushi mushi."
The trunks arrived yesterday.
As soon as Mom finds them,
I'll send your roller skates.
Sorry I haven't written more often,
but you know me. How's life
at Sacred Heart this week?

School's okay. Here's a map I drew
of the Balkan Peninsula. I got an A,
I respond, trying to make my capitals like his,
and no mistakes with the Esterbrook pen
Gram gave me when we left the States.
Yesterday Miriam Yamaguchi
and I won a three-legged race.
Today is Reverend Mother's Feast Day.
At four o'clock we'll have tea and cake.
When can I come home?

Then because it's Sunday afternoon,
time to stay in bed, rest, read, write letters,
but not talk, I do what I do every Sunday
afternoon: drop the unsealed letter
into Mother Maher's locked box, return
to my futon, and watch Marilyn Fu,
whose tatami mat is next to mine.

Marilyn is Chinese. I love the way
she parts her long black hair down the middle,
and clips it back with two barrettes.
And I love the way she turns her paper
sideways, dips her writing brush into ink,
and while holding it straight up and down,
instead of writing on the lines, stroke
by delicate stroke, fills each column
with tiny works of art, top to bottom, right
to left.

A Year in San Juan

We'd barely unpacked, when Dad came home
with the news: another reassignment.
And before I knew it I was leaning
over the rail of the balcony waving good-bye,
and Mom was inside smoking a cigarette,
Gypsies! That's what he thinks we are, gypsies!
The only thing your father cares about
is that goddamned job. Go ahead. Wave.
This time, you and I are staying put!

Most nights it was light before I heard the key.
If Mom was singing "Dance, Ballerina Dance,"
I knew she'd seen Nat King Cole
whose face was on an easel in the lobby
of the Condado Beach Hotel.
"Oh, My Papa" meant Eddie Fisher was in town.

Mornings I'd get myself off to Santa Teresita,
then afternoons after school, catch the bus
back to the Hotel La Concha, where I'd change
into my black nylon tank suit and swim laps
while Carlos strode the edge of the pool,
blowing his whistle and clicking his stopwatch.

If Mom wasn't in the casino playing blackjack
or craps, she'd be sunbathing, ordering
gin and tonics from the waiter who walked
between terry-cloth covered lounge chairs
balancing a tray of drinks. Mom loved it
whenever a hotel guest said, *Nice tan.*
How long you been here?

Then she could say, *Oh, three, four months,*
and let them think she was a rich divorcée,
not a married woman with an apartment
down the street, who had free membership
because I was on the swim team.

On Saturday nights the hotel put on beach parties.
They lit torches, dug a pit in the sand,
and roasted a pig. A steel band played
from the back of a pickup. The smoke
and smell of burning rose through the palm trees,
and I'd mingle with the tourists, drink rum punch,
do the limbo, and jump on the trampoline.

It was 1958. *Life* magazine
was doing an article on Puerto Rico.
The photographer watched me jump.
I could stay in the air for a long time,
so he paid me a dollar, aimed his lights upwards,
and took my picture.
His name was Don.
The next day we rode horseback at a resort
near El Yunque, the rain forest. It was fun.
Over dinner he looked at me closely.
How old are you? he said.
Eleven, I said.
I didn't see him again, but in the picture
you can tell it's me jumping,
and you can see the roof line of La Concha.
It's shaped like a giant seashell, and all lit up.

All those months Carlos would say,
Swimmers, take your mark!—
and I'd wait for the crack of the gun,
then reach through the air, pull my arms

through the water. Backstroke was my best event.
I usually won a ribbon.
And at night, when I let myself in,
the same Sinatra album would be lying
on the couch, the same lizard on the ceiling.
The air always smelled like perfume
and stale cigarettes, and I'd fall asleep
looking out the window, wondering
how Dad was doing, if it was today
or tomorrow in the Philippines.

Sometimes she'd be gone for days.
I knew she had a boyfriend—the way you know,
but not really. Then she started hinting
about moving in with him, saying things like,
How'd you like to live in a house on the beach?
I said, *Not even for one second*—I'd write to Dad
and tell, move in with Carlos and his sisters.

I don't know what did it, but shortly later
we moved to Manila.
First though, we had a vacation in Honolulu.
We stayed at the Hilton Hawaiian Village Hotel
on Waikiki Beach. Tennessee Ernie Ford was there.
Mom tipped the pool boy a lot of money
to put our beach chairs next to his,
and all day long she kept singing
"Sixteen Tons and Whaddaya Get."

The Elizabeth Taylor Look-Alike Contest
Manila, 1960

I'd never heard of that contest
till Mom showed me a *Manila Times*

with my face above two Filipinos.
Mom said she thought I knew

she'd sent in my photo, and why
would anyone call it cheating?

Was it her fault Elizabeth Taylor
didn't look Filipino?

Mom just thought I shouldn't slouch
at the opening of *Butterfield 8.*

That's when I'd model the prizes:
a custom-made dress by Consuelo,

makeover by Alfonso. Mom said,
Everyone knows he's the best

hairdresser in town. Well, I didn't
think so. Not after the mess

he made of my hair, that mole,
and my makeup—all of it lavender!

And Consuelo, what was she thinking?
The contortions I went through

getting into that dress! And that's when

Mom told me I couldn't see the movie.

After they announced my name
and I walked on stage, I'd have to wait

in the lobby till the curtain came down,
because Elizabeth Taylor played

a prostitute, and I was twelve.

Stop It!

It lasted only seconds, but they were long
and indelible, so as my hand drifts to my head,
I see Muffy in the Girls Room
at the American School in Manila.
I was new, but I'd noticed her right away.
Her hair—who could miss it? Thick and long,
and every shade of gold. In Algebra
I sat behind her, watched it shine and change color.
Now I stood at the next sink and watched
her examine herself in the mirror.
And when she leaned close to it,
then closer, the hunger in her eyes
grabbed hold of me. In First Grade
when Sister held up the statue
of Mary inside the little blue grotto,
and announced, *Whoever's best this week*
will win it! I didn't just want that statue,
I wanted to *be* Mary. She was all I could see.
Now I couldn't take my eyes off Muffy.
I fed off, and followed her gaze.
And when she grasped the wayward hair
that she'd been staring at, wrapped it
around and around her finger,
and with the same tension
I'm now applying to this unruly strand,
pulled it out of her scalp, something of her
went into me. And I was changed.
Why? Again and again, I've woken
to what I'm doing, looked at the strand
of lifeless hair in my hand, and begged to know.
And not knowing, I've examined the root—

the shiny white bulb at the end
of a successful pull, and thought,
if there was no avoiding this—
if this urge, this need, this bad habit,
whatever you want to call it—this curse?—
was always inside me, asleep in some gene,
or crease in my brain, waiting, waiting,
for what?—Muffy?—adolescence?—
the right cue to set it going?—like that egg
which had just recently slipped out
and left its burgundy stain—
oh why couldn't this have been delayed?
Then I wouldn't have gone home
from school that day—home to that house
we'd just rented—sat alone in the living room,
and in the armchair under the ceiling fan,
pulled and pulled till my head hurt,
till my scalp was covered with dots of blood,
till I was in such a frenzy
I didn't see my father in the doorway.
My father, bless his restless soul,
all I ever wanted was for him to notice me.
And now I've yanked my hand
down to my lap. But too late. He's seen.
And now he's seen the billowy
tumbleweed on the floor.
Why are you doing that?
I still don't have an answer.
Well stop it, he says. *Can't you stop it?*
Go back to biting your nails?

My Father's Voice

That rare night together ended
with Mom asleep in the front seat,
me forgotten in back, and Dad,
a little intoxicated, I think,
driving home from the Officers Club.
I remember the wet sheen of that black
volcanic rock, the rough slide
of pebbles washed by the sea,
the few scattered stars, and the glow
of his cigar that seemed lit by them.
And oh, I remember the slight lean
of his head as he began to sing
with a longing so deep
I held my breath and followed him
to his mother's land in a distant sea.
And though I could only make out
the wave of blond hair along the back
of his godlike head, I pierced the curve
of his neck, till through his clear
tenor voice I saw the rounded white collar
and big red bow around the throat
of a ten-year-old choir boy standing
next to his mother outside their cold-water flat.
And oh, now I remember, slowing down,
that turn in the road, our darkened bungalow,
my own silent voice, *Oh no, not yet!*
as he glanced at my mother,
and I shut my eyes, till like mercy
that car drove on for one last spin,

another round of "When Irish Eyes Are Smiling,"
and I filled myself up with the blessing
of that sound, the thick cigar smoke,
knowing tomorrow he'd leave us again.

Hong Kong

1.

The one time Mom took me to Hong Kong
I thought we were going to shop
for gold bracelets, then come home
like she always did—bearing gifts.
But a man was inside our hotel room.
And when she called him *Honey*,
I sat stone-faced on the edge of my bed.
My eyes followed her into the bathroom,
stared at that door, the air thick with the sound
of her brushing her teeth, him crossing, un-
crossing his legs, shifting around in his seat,
till she stood in the light, so bright it hurt,
everything around her as white as her body, moving
under the veil of her gown, teasing,
Want to stay over?

The next morning she started in: *You're visiting
from boarding school. Dad and I are divorced. Understand?*
I did.
So that night at her party, I scanned
the round table of faces, and when I found
Honey's, I set out to undo them.
My mother and father are married, I said.
For a moment it was quiet.
Then his eyes on mine, he stood up,
walked over, and politely pulled out my chair.
With me by the hand, he walked toward
the dance floor. I remember they were playing
"La Vie En Rose," and I thought, *Now what?*

Are we going to dance?
But we kept going, and for the next hour
or so, my mother's lover and I walked
the dark streets of that city. I knew
I'd be in for it, knew my father—everyone
called him a *saint*—would expect me
to take it: *Be kind to your mother.*
She can't help herself.
But I kept saying, *My mother and father*
are married. We live in Manila.
We live in Manila.

2.

Let's go, I said. But Mom didn't want to.
She turned to the sailor, said, *Do me a favor.*
And now, decades later, sometimes
even in sleep, I still follow my footsteps
along the sidewalk, in the street, through
puddles and broken glass, past rickshaws,
and dogs sniffing trash. I see myself,
a young girl, going fast, careful
not to look at him as we walk
past windows filled with pink neon tubes
outlining martini glasses and women
with big pointy breasts. I remember
how strange it felt when we turned
a corner and I saw the gated shop
where just that morning she'd bought
jade cufflinks for Dad, and a little farther,
the Peninsula Hotel, where I pretended
not to notice when he stumbled
over the curb, then lurched as the doorman
opened the plate-glass door
and we stepped into the lobby

where I should've stayed put,
should've marched right up to the woman
behind the desk. Of course I blame Mom,
but shouldn't I have known?
That's what weighs on me each time
I see him bent over, reeking of whiskey,
see me fumbling for the key, pushing
him away. How I managed to get past him
and let myself in is a mystery,
but I can still feel my shoulder leaning
into that door, pushing and pushing
against his weight, pushing and pushing
until I couldn't push any more.

On the Outskirts of Manila

How old were we? I was fifteen. He, sixteen.
Or, maybe a bit younger, since I would
have been wearing my bracelet—the little
gold ID bracelet he gave me that birthday,
with *Christine* engraved on the flat surface,
Love, Paqui on the side against my skin.
We were inside the American Military Cemetery
standing amid acres of manicured lawns,
and row upon row of white wooden crosses
and six-pointed stars, at the center
of a copse of exotic plants and trees
behind a stand of flowering pink hibiscus.
We were kissing.
It can't have been the first time we'd gone there—
taken the long walk from the Polo Club,
where we spent every free minute
swimming, playing tennis, or holding hands,
wandering around paddocks and stables,
looking for, but rarely finding
a secluded place to kiss.
I can still feel the sun—that tropical
torch which seemed to burn everything in.
The hum of insects. The not-too-distant groan
of that lawn mower. My anxiety.
Him. Him. Him. His smell.
He always smelled of lavender,
a scent I still can't breathe
without his face coming into focus,
and his hands—slim and fine—the way his fingers
undid the buttons of my blouse, unhooked
my bra. It all comes back to me—how we stood

45

facing each other: chest-naked, near,
but not so near that he couldn't see
my breasts. And as he began touching them,
I moved closer, and for the first time
through his clothing and mine, I felt
his penis swell and grow hard,
his body quiver.
When we finally stepped apart
I noticed a small wet spot near the zipper
on his light gray—I think they were gray—
cotton slacks. At first I wasn't sure
what it was—but then, embarrassed, I turned
my head—and on the ground, I saw my blouse—
as green as the emerald grass,
with those miniature sprays of white roses
printed on it—lying there, emptied
and still.

Lavender

From where I sat, on other nights,
I'd play charades, listen
to the Everly Brothers sing
those corny tunes you don't forget,
and if just the two of us were there, kiss.
But on this night, after what I'd naively
believed would never end, had ended—
after the tears, the loss of weight,
after I tore so much hair out of my head
a bald spot appeared—
while the boy I loved took a Filipino
girl to a party, I sat on that rattan
love seat alone, holding myself very still,
saying good-bye to his mother,
and to the hours stretched over years
I'd spent inside that room. Good-bye
to the large round table with the lazy Susan
I loved to spin; good-bye to the smooth
stone floor where little Nenunca once played
with her pet rabbit while I showed her brother
steps kids on *American Band Stand* did;
and outside the always open patio doors:
good-bye to the garden; good-bye
to the star apple tree; good-bye
to the empty rabbit cage.
And all the while, sitting across from me
in her piña dress and blue pearls,
Mrs. Ortigas kept offering
to have Ahu bring me a little something
to eat, a cup of tea; kept shaking
her well-coifed head, saying, *It's better this way.*

You'll see. You'll move back to the States soon.
You'll go to college. You'll meet
a nice American boy. You'll see.
But I'm forty-nine today. And the truth is,
after the marriages, divorces, illnesses
and deaths; after the years of therapy,
Prozac and Amitriptyline,
though I've stopped searching for Paqui
wherever I go, stopped seeing him
in the shape of one man's nose, the outline
of another's chin, stopped irrationally
checking phone books in airports and cities
around the world for Ortigas, Francisco M.,
I still pull out my hair;
and if I walk into a store and see
a bottle of Yardley's English Lavender,
I split in two: part of me wants to turn
and run out the door;
the other part—the part that always wins—
wants to go up to it, loosen the cap,
and haunt myself with the scent of his skin.

Chapter Three

First Wedding

Still hoping the carefully addressed
invitation
had served its only purpose
before stepping up to the altar
Saturday
the Fourth of June
Nineteen Hundred and Sixty-Six
Eleven in the morning
I glanced over my shoulder
looking for the
one
I'd prayed would come
to his senses
fly here and
stop
this service

Two Continents

When someone called to say that you
were getting married on the other side
of the world, to a girl whose name
I remembered, in a church down the street
from the balcony where we once stood
vowing never to part, I was standing
in a room where we never were.
The floor was white linoleum with gold
veins running through it. The appliances
were green, and a yellow dishtowel
hung on a hook by the sink.
It was June 4, 1968. That night
I did what I always did: retraced scenes
of our years together—only if possible,
more vividly, in greater detail.

When the clock radio went off at six
the next morning, the newsman said
Robert Kennedy had been shot.
Everyone at work went around with long faces.
Which was strange, because five years before,
the night we broke up—on that balcony—
of course I couldn't sleep,
and when the morning paper came,
the headline said, JFK SHOT DEAD.
All of Manila cried that day: servants,
the Chinese ladies downstairs, jeepney drivers,
even the little boy with betel nut stained teeth
and American tennis shoes, who sold
hand-painted pink ivory fans scented with sandalwood,
under the banyan tree, in front of that church
down the street.

Expecting

You can't fool me, Mom said, *I know*
he's there. If I have to I'll do it again.
She was talking about my father
who wasn't there, and from whom she was divorced,
but living with, when she wasn't living
with Dick, which was most of the time.
And she was referring to my tires
which she'd slashed, causing me to stay awake
at night, worrying she would show up
and do it again. Or worse.
So after I hung up the phone,
I went out for the day.
I spent the morning at the paint store
looking through wallpaper books,
and in the afternoon, still afraid
to go home, I gave in to an urge
for a chocolate chip ice cream cone.
At Howard Johnson's an old woman held
the door open. *Don't hurry, dear*, she said
as I came up the walk, and when I got there,
she smiled, and patted my swollen belly.

Even Now

Every so often when I look at my daughter,
I see, not my ex-husband whom she resembles,
but a man I haven't seen for over
twenty-five years. It's an old story. Married,
though not to each other, we shared an office,
attraction, talk of discontent. I remember
a party—someone's promotion?—the two of us
dancing. It must have been after that,
we began using work as an excuse to stay late.
Leaving in two cars, we'd park one
at a nearby strip mall, then drive to nowhere
in particular, or to a small restaurant
in Cold Spring Harbor, before circling back.
Truth is, though I would have, and though
there were weighings and longings,
we didn't become lovers.
With experience I lacked, he said,
If it weren't for my son . . .

And so, hoping to save my own marriage,
though it took my husband and me many months
to conceive, after a long labor
aided by forceps, our daughter was born.
Blotchy, scratched, it was love at first sight.
Yet looking back at myself cradling her
that first morning, her gaze so penetrating,
I can still feel the swell of guilt
as I found myself thinking of him,
the sense of tiredness as I resisted
the urge to pick up the phone at my bedside—
his presence absorbing me, hauling at me,

till a week later, I dressed Nicole in a tiny
pink hat and sweater, left our home and drove those
sixteen miles down the highway.
Even now I can hear the slight rustling
of leaves as I crossed that carpet of grass,
then walked toward the full-length
window which was our—now *his*
office—third from the left. Closer now,
I can see him getting up from his desk,
the complexity of emotions moving
through his face as he stood at that window,
and like the nurse in the hospital nursery
once did for her father, I held my infant
daughter up close to the glass.

Picture Perfect

In those days, after putting the baby
down for a nap, I'd tidy up.
And when there was no toy out of place,
no dish unwashed, no speck of dust
on the white kitchen counter or floor,
no smudge on the piano, no fingerprints
on the windows, glass-topped tables,
or patio doors, I'd stare at the phone.
Sometimes I'd open the drawer under it,
take out the Yellow Pages,
and look up "psychiatrist."
Once or twice I started to dial.
But the thought of exposing
so much disarray would send me
outdoors, past tubs filled with jasmine
to the lounge chair by the pool overlooking
the dock with the gleaming white boat
tied up to it. And whoever happened
to sail by, notice the scent of jasmine,
and glance up, would see me sitting there,
tanned and pretty in my straw hat
and bikini, sipping iced tea with ice cubes
made of lemonade and springs of mint,
looking perfectly happy.

They Knew

That summer in Florida
when my two-year-old sat in the booster chair
while the woman trimming her hair
asked her her name, the name of her dolly,
and how many fingers old she was,
I sat in the next booth looking into
the mirror, one eye on them, the other
on the hairdresser working on me.
And at the first hint that she'd discovered
the thin patches, and short, broken
strands near the crown of my head,
I met her eyes in the glass. *I lost some hair*
after my daughter was born.
It's been a little slow growing back in,
but the doctor says that's common,
a hormone imbalance, that sort of thing, I said,
half-following what I was saying,
thinking that what I'd intended to say
was coming out smoothly enough,
half-wishing I hadn't lied,
then instead of hopping from salon
to salon, or cutting my own hair,
I could come back to this shop.
And the scabs? she asked.
My scalp itches sometimes, I said,
trying to keep the clearest look of innocence.
A good sign, don't you think? It probably means
new hairs are pushing through.
But feeling overwhelmed now, and thinking
she knew, I averted my eyes and said,

Hi Sweetie, oh, don't you look pretty,
and got all involved with Nicole
and with what was going on over there.
But if my demeanor implied anything
like ease, that too, was untrue.
So after I paid and handed out tips,
and the receptionist handed Nicole
the lollipop she'd been promised,
and we were back out in the mall,
I headed to the bookstore,
and to the Medical Dictionary
I'd paused and looked up at
when I'd been in there browsing.
And now, done with vacillating
and needing to see if there was anything in it
about this habit—this odious habit
I believed was peculiar to me—about *me*—
I took the heavy book
down from the shelf,
looked up "hair" in the index,
scanned below, and surprised to see
"hair pulling (Trichotillomania)"
turned to the page,
and felt the world fall away.

Trichotillomania: Involuntary hair pulling. A primary psychiatric disorder, it is characterized by the repeated urge to pull out scalp hair, eyelashes, eyebrows or other body hair. Mean age of onset: 13.2 years. The cause is largely unknown, but ruptures in the mother-infant bond and maternal deprivation in early life are indicated. The majority of patients are female.

For a moment I closed my eyes.
Then I put the book back,

and with my daughter now asleep
in her stroller, I left the store, frightened,
confused, both renouncing what I'd read,
and wondering how they knew.

The One Lie

The men I've had sex with would not
be worth noting, but for the fact
that three of my four involvements
took place at once: Phil, my then husband;
Jonas, the dyslexic artist who smelled of Brut,
who only God knows why I later married;
and Dr. Pesek, the so-called therapist, who,
rather than help me through the mess
I was already in, spent all our sessions
crying to me about *his* loneliness,
then invited me to his house for dinner
and a swim. Needless to say, it was life
gone amuck: surges and furies, meetings
on the sly, evasions, accusations, denials
and deceits—a series of lies, which now,
over twenty years later, I might recall
with less sting, but for the one
all the others came to. The lie I told
my unsuspecting four-year-old daughter,
when, unable to even hint at divorce,
or say anything close to the truth,
as I was about to take her away
from her father, friends, and lovely home
on a deepwater canal two blocks
from the sea, and move to the not-quite-rough,
but shabby neighborhood, and furnished
apartment I'd rented at the end
of a dead-end street, I said only
that I'd found us a cute little place
of our own so we could walk to the beach.

The Artist

It was the usual argument: Jonas insisting
he wasn't a lying, cheating, double-crossing
scoundrel who chased every skirt in sight.
He was an artist—a French Moroccan Abstract Expressionist.
Unlike me, his uptight American wife,
he wasn't hung up about sex.
And that's where we left it.
Where we always left it.

But this time those words stayed with me.
When I woke. When I slept.
The night of our party, when I smiled
as two hundred guests leaned toward me:
You must be so proud of your husband.
That man has such talent. You're so lucky
to be married to an artist.

They were there when I danced with the off-
duty cop—the one with the beautiful smile,
hired to keep his eyes on the paintings.
In fact, those words were still with me
when I swallowed a few magic mushrooms,
led the soon silly cop past the hibiscus,
behind the night-blooming jasmine,
to a quiet corner of our yard, where after
telling him, *Relax. It's okay.*
I'm married to an artist—
a French Moroccan Abstract Expressionist,
we lay ourselves down on the just mowed grass,
began making love, and kept on,
and didn't stop.

Crimes and Misdemeanors

After months of counseling, Dr. Coursin
finally turns to my husband, says, *Jonas,*
you need to find your locus of control.
And Jonas says, *Locust?*
A locust is a grasshopper.
And I jump up, about to say, *That's it!*
It's over!
But this scene reminds me of a Woody Allen movie.
And I'm laughing out loud, thinking,
Woody kind of looks like a grasshopper.
Before you know it, I'm in a full-blown
laughing jag. I can't stop.
Then it occurs to me how much that creep
reminds me of Jonas. Except smarter.
How neither has any morals.
How I hate myself for watching his movies
after I swore I'd stop. How hard it must be
for poor Mia—come to think of it—
poor *me.* Now I'm on the sofa sobbing,
remembering our party. That model.
Their little jokes. His hand on her thigh.
The nights out. The lies, lies, lies.
And I'm thinking all sorts of things,
like murder. How to do it? Poison?
A bullet in his chest?
Better yet, rip his heart out. There must be
a version of a heart in there. Somewhere.
Should I drop a hint, say, *Sweetheart . . .*
something special . . . tomorrow . . . ?
Now I'm laughing again—holding my sides.

Jonas is giving Dr. Coursin that
see-what-I-have-to-live-with look,
and Dr. Coursin's handing me tissues,
saying, *Time's up.*

Diagnosis

1.

The change was so gradual,
we hardly noticed.
Then a friend he hadn't seen in a while said,
Jonas, you don't sound right,
so my husband, a nonsmoker,
went to our local physician
who wrote a prescription, and told him
to gargle.
But his voice grew hoarser
and weaker,
so he went to a doctor in Concord
who scraped a tiny piece of flesh
from his larynx and sent it to Boston.
The biopsy report came back *negative.*
But his voice grew hoarser
and weaker,
so he went to an otolaryngologist
in Philadelphia who coaxed,
swallow, swallow,
and I watched the monitor,
followed the laryngoscope
down the pulsing
wet pink of his throat
to the vocal chord
that would not move
anymore.

2.

And when the oncologist promised him *hell*:
intravenous infusions of cisplatin, radiation,

a possible laryngectomy, followed by
a *reasonable chance* at life, what he called *hope*—
I let go of the past—the accusations,
threats, and tears—and moved closer.
But he'd have none of it. He turned
to a younger woman—a *healer*—
our house filling up with Chinese herbs,
her smell, bills. They rode bicycles together.
They paddled a canoe. I know this
because I saw them. And he looked at me
accusingly, said, *This malignancy*
means someone's strangling me.
So the next morning, when I overheard him
talking on the phone, barely able
to whisper, *I don't care how much it costs,*
charge me double, charge me triple,
we can catch a flight today,
I didn't ask questions, not even *where?*
I went into our bedroom closet, took down
our suitcases, and began to pack.
But when he came up behind me
and rasped, *I didn't mean YOU,*
that was it. I called him, *liar.*
I called him, *cheater.*
I called him, *hopeless.*

Medication

I changed my mind, I said
phoning Dr. Coursin at 3:00 a.m.
Can you write me a prescription, NOW, please?
And after a few weeks on Prozac
the little silver gun inside my head
disappeared. And after a few weeks more,
instead of moping on the couch
watching the birds watch me pull out my hair,
I filled the empty feeder,
then faced the stack of bills
I'd been scared to look at
since our insurance company went bankrupt
the same week Jonas, my husband of fifteen years,
finished his chemotherapy, and ran off
to Italy with Catherine, his therapist
whom I couldn't stand even before
I knew they were lovers, in search of
his inner child they called *little Jerry,*
leaving me the debt he said was mine
because I caused his cancer
by paying the monthly premiums
on this policy I knew he didn't want,
since according to *his* knowledge of karma
(which I was too stupid to understand)
health insurance guarantees disease.
Like David Letterman says,
You can't make this stuff up.
But thank God someone invented
whatever's inside those green and yellow capsules
I didn't want, but now swallowed religiously,
because besides helping me

do what I used to do, like eat and sleep,
and cook and clean, and paint
the picture frames I made for a living,
and travel to craft shows,
and mow the lawn, and shovel snow,
and visit my daughter at college,
and my dad in the nursing home,
and my mom in the loony bin,
and file for yet another divorce—
I made phone call after phone call,
and Xeroxed bills, and wrote letters,
and a year or so later,
Notices of Payment
began to arrive in the mail
as the State of New Hampshire
paid every doctor and hospital
every dollar of the tens of thousands owed.
But I still pulled out my hair.
So now Dr. Coursin and I discussed
what to do about my trichotillomania,
the treatment-resistant disorder
I've had since childhood.
And since I'd just gone off Prozac
and didn't want to take another drug,
I said, *Can we try behavioral therapy?*
And he said, *Sure,*
then told me to lift up a hank of my hair
and show him where I pulled from.
And I said, *oh,*
then just sat there not lifting a finger,
painfully aware of that place
right below his neck—that V of flesh
I found erotic and tried not to look at
whenever he unbuttoned his collar, and
that I was tearing up, something

I hadn't been able to do on Prozac.
Have you ever exposed a bald spot before?
Not on purpose.
Would it be like undressing?
Yes.
Then don't, he said. *But someday,*
when you meet the right man, Christine—
one who respects and protects you—
don't keep this part of yourself secret.
Show him. Let him kiss it.

Chapter Four

Two Certainties

I don't know why Mom let him in,
but she did, and the IRS man said,
Ma'am, it can't go on like this.
So Mom showed him the shopping bags,
suitcases, and shoeboxes stuffed
with statements and receipts.
Be my guest, she said. *My husband
has Alzenheimer's disease*—a mispronounced
fact Mom used successfully to avoid things
like traffic tickets and lines at the bank—
Excuse me, my husband has Alzenheimer's disease.
But the IRS man wasn't impressed.
*Sorry to hear that, ma'am. Nevertheless,
you have all this income.*
And that's when Mom lost it.
*Young man, it's not income. It's interest.
I've never worked a day in my life.*

JOE I

Dad's sitting next to me at the breakfast table.
We're eating Rice Krispies.
He's reading the box.
I'm turning the pages of my favorite Golden Book.
Dad takes the shiny steel pencil
from his shirt pocket, twists it till the lead
comes out, and under the picture of Bugs Bunny
eating birthday carrot cake in his underground house,
draws a small circle around the word "to."
This will be your job today, he says,
find and circle all the "to's." The next day
he circles "the," then "and."

*

Dad, what do you enjoy most?
Learning.

*

I was eleven, Dad says, repeating the story
he told me five minutes ago. *We were sitting
around the kitchen table playing cards.
My mother said, "Who wants sweets?"
I said "Me!"
On the way to the pantry she danced
that little jig she always did, then dropped
to the floor. Pop said, "Oh God, get the priest!"
So I ran to St. Joseph's—didn't genuflect,
light a candle, anything—just raced down the aisle,
across the altar, out the sacristy.
At the rectory, I banged on every door. Empty.*

71

By the time I got home, she was gone.
Pop said, "The angels came and took her away."
Then Dad tears up again: *I still think it was my fault.*

*

After two weeks of tests Dad sits on the edge
of his chair, directly in front
of the doctor's desk. A plastic brain
sits on top of it. I sit a little to the side.
I watch my father from the corner
of my eye. He looks like a schoolboy
waiting to be told if he's passed.
The doctor says, *Remember the blocks*
that we were just putting together?
It was very difficult for you.

J.M.J.

After the doctor said that Dad had
what I'd suspected, but Dad said
he had no symptoms of, we sat down together
to straighten out his checkbook.
At first his numbers agreed with the bank's,
then in the middle of September,
everything went haywire.
He'd written his license plate number, CBR343,
where the car payment should've been,
a few random zeros, then something
incomprehensible, followed by a long
red arrow that pointed to JOE,
printed in block letters which took me back
to Sister Rose's fifth-grade class,
and my desk, third row from the front,
at the end, by the window.

I was good at school. But on that day,
when Sister Rose said, *Number one:*
if eight thousand four hundred and twelve
is the dividend, and the divisor
is ninety-seven point thirty-five,
what is the quotient?
everything I ever knew, flew out of my head.
Before I could figure out what to do,
Sister was saying, *Number two,*
and I was floating, looking down
at the back of my head bent over that page,
blank, except where I'd written my name,
and J.M.J. for Jesus, Mary and Joseph,
and at the same time, I was sitting there

73

next to my father, looking at his blank face,
reaching for his hand, and for one
long second I was holding everything—
all of it, in my mind, all at once.

JOE II

Dad kneels beside his father's casket,
studies the face and snow white hair
of this man he so resembles, leans closer
to examine the White Owl cigar
Uncle Jack had slipped into the breast pocket
of Pop's one good suit.
Can't quite place him, Dad says.
But you can tell he was a big shot.

*

That's not my ceiling, Dad says, looking up
from his nursing home bed.
We had to change it, Dad.
How come?
The roof fell in.
Oh, Lord! he says. *Is everyone okay?*
So far so good, I say.
Thank God, he says.

*

This time I spot Dad sitting at the end
of a long hallway, his blue hospital gown
half off. He's waving to me, his thin arm
high in the air, gesturing, *Come on down!*
Halfway there I see he's diapered,
tied to an armchair. He points
to his cheek, puckers his lips. Happy
he still recognizes me, I lean down,
wrap my arms around his neck,
kiss his unshaved face, then turn

to pull up a chair.
And when I look back, he's waving
to a stranger.

*

Dad's slumped in his wheelchair.
I straighten him. Wipe drool from his chin.
I say his name. Write it on an erasable board.
I hold the board in what I hope
is his line of vision. I say his name again.

A Better Place

1.

The aide asks us to leave the room
while she bathes Dad, changes his diaper
and bedding. Outside the closed door
Mom whispers, *Most of the help here*
are black, you know. But you shouldn't judge
a person by the color of their skin.
As she's saying this a nurse walks by
pushing a medicine cart. *He's gay*, Mom says,
under her breath. *Can't you tell?*
Mr. Howard down the hall—well,
his wife complained. But I said, Live and let live.
What's that expression—To each his own?
Now back inside the large, bright room,
Dad's clean shaven, a new coverlet
pulled up to his chin. Mom leans over,
studies the uncluttered face of this man
whose mind has traveled far from this bed.
Tell me the truth, Chrissy, she says.
What should we do? Should we move Dad
to a better place?

2.

And now someone's disconnected
your feeding tube. They've pushed the IV rack
to the corner of the room, unplugged the cord
and left it dangling.
Dad, I remember when you ate sandwiches
made with thick curls of purple onion,
Swiss cheese and mustard between slices

of seeded rye bread—when you sat
propped and harnessed so as not to slide
out of your wheelchair and I fed you
ice cream with a tiny flat wooden spoon.
You couldn't talk, but your eyes told me
you liked it. Now I don't know what's going on
in your head. With your eyelids stuck shut,
your fingers clenched, your mind shot,
I don't know if I should walk down the hall
to the nurses station—remind them to bring
a new bag of Ensure and plug you back in,
or ask God's forgiveness, and leave.

Dad's Funeral

At the last minute Mom changes her mind.
There will be no satin-lined casket.
She wants Dad cremated, his ashes
placed in Lake Myosotis.

Inside the church, I smell lilies,
hear my sister-in-law singing.
One hundred and fifty friends and family
have gathered: Tommy Wansboro,
Rosemary Kissane—Mom points out
Gig Bullman, Dad's friend since second grade,
others we haven't seen in years.

At the altar, Father O'Neil asks,
Where's the deceased?
I hold out the can. Mumble
an apology, the change in plans.
Father gives me a look, a whispered lecture.
The Albany Diocese forbids ashes
in churches. They accept only bodies—
whole or in part. Would I please put
Mr. Korfhage back in the car.

Mom's collapsed. No. She's dropped
to her knees, giving me the eye, planting
big kisses on Father O'Neil's finger,
where, were he a bishop he'd be wearing
a ring, which of course, he isn't—
an obvious ploy, which makes him so mad,
he throws up his hands, which the congregation
takes to mean, *All rise.*

Widow

After Dad died, Mom didn't eat or sleep,
almost never brushed her teeth, or changed
out of her bathrobe. She just lay on the couch,
weeping, fingering her rosary,
watching the O. J. Simpson murder trial,
a habit she formed during Dad's final months,
when she spent mornings at the nursing home,
picking fights with the staff, then afternoons
in bed, watching television.
One day I came in to find her bustling
around the kitchen. She'd bathed, fixed her hair,
put on clean clothes and lipstick.
I've got so much to tell you, she said.

*

The last time Mom let loose at my house
the man from Sears was installing a new
dishwasher. Mom started throwing things:
china, glasses, my Calyx Ware teapot.
The man was kneeling on the floor,
dodging maybe, but otherwise acting
like nothing was happening.
I was against the refrigerator.
I think I kept closing my eyes.
All I could hear was him connecting hoses,
tightening screws, the sound of dishes,
that dial spinning through cycles,
water going on, off; on, off;
Mom screaming, *Cunt, whore, cold-hearted bitch.*
My voice, *Stop. Please stop.*

Then Mom was on the floor, dropped
like a bag of groceries, leaning
into the man's shoulder.
No one knows, she kept saying,
No one knows.

*

I'm using Mom's phone to make a local call.
Leave a quarter on the kitchen table, she says.
Everything will be yours once I'm dead.

*

The medevac nurse adjusts the long
plastic tubes that carry oxygen
and fluids in and out of my mother.
He wraps the Velcro cuff around her arm,
pumps it up, checks her blood pressure,
then presses his fingers into her wrist,
takes her pulse. *Louise, squeeze my hand
if you can hear me,* he says. *You're on
a portable respirator now.* Turning aside,
he lifts the lid on the small metal box
strapped to the back of the navigator's seat.
Now what can I do for you, he says to me,
heart, kidney, or Pepsi?

Freebies

Airplane pillows, eyeshades, towels marked *Hilton,*
Sheraton, tiny toiletries, mini jars
of marmalade, silverware, Bibles—
I'd stuff them into trash bags, drive to the dump,
and think of Mom—her last weeks
on life support, and leading up to them,
our trip to the islands.
Her hands shook.
Her lips were almost blue.
Yet, that first night at the Hyatt in Aruba
she couldn't rest till she called the front desk.
This is Mrs. Korfhage.
No. Not Corsage. Korfhage.
K - O - R - F as in Frank - H - A - G as in George - E.
I don't care what the reservation says.
We were promised ocean FRONT, not ocean VIEW.
What a pip, I'd think, remembering
how I overtipped the bellhop
for what we both knew she'd been after—
a gift basket filled with tropical fruit,
a bottle of champagne,
discounts for spa services,
and fifty $1 gambling chips.
Bless her. On past trips Mom would get up
at dawn, reserve a lounge chair under
an umbrella with her beach coat and sandals,
then after returning to the room
for another snooze, a few cups of Sanka,
and breakfast in bed, spend the rest
of the day sunbathing, lolling in the sea,
or shopping for duty-free perfumes

and Lladro figurines.
This time she mostly slept.
At night, though, after the masseuse finished
Mom's rubdown, I'd help her
into one of my dresses I'd loaned her
and never got back, and off we'd go
to the casino.

Looking back, I suppose it shouldn't have come
as such a shock when six weeks later
I answered the phone and heard a doctor say
Mom was in Intensive Care.
But just like the more she sipped free drinks,
nibbled free canapés, and played roulette
with free chips, the more she seemed to improve,
I couldn't tell if all Mom's trips to doctors
and hospitals were because she was sick,
or because even after Dad died
his GE benefits provided her free medical.

Mom's Last Notes to Me and Herself

(*found inside Willowwood Nursing Home, Williamstown, MA, after Mom's death on August 15, 1996*)

DON'T SELL THE HOUSE
      IT'S MY ACE IN THE HOLE

What I like about myself
      I have a Roman nose
      I am a kind person
      I have feelings for people (not relatives)
      I loved taking care of my house, car, Joe, etc.
      I don't worry about my looks so long as I'm clean
      My pictures are all in albums
      I pray to God daily

What have you been up to?
      DON'T SELL GENERAL ELECTRIC

What I like about myself
      Creativity
            i.e. Buy things
            such as a harvest table to put pottery on
      Always willing to listen and to learn
            i.e. Jeopardy
            A&E Biography
                  Churchill
                  Roosevelt
                  Kennedy
            I read Rose Kennedy's autobiography
            I have no racial discrimination

I love the good earth. I'll always want to be
gardening even if I can't.

my hand is shaky

DON'T LET PAT IN THE HOUSE

Don't talk using up air

Chapter Five

Nicole E-mails from Cambodia

I can't carry money here, I give it all away.
Today a boy came up to me—
he couldn't have been more than ten.
I think his jaw was abscessed. It was bound
with a kerchief—a dirty rag.
He asked where I was from.
When I said, "America,"
He said slowly, pronouncing every syllable,
"I know all about your country.
The capital is Washington, DC.
Alaska is the largest state.
Two hundred seventy million people live there.
Everyone is rich." Then he grinned.
His teeth were rotten—little black stubs.
I suppose it was an experienced smile,
meant for me to pity him.
But it was beautiful, Mom.
Do you know what I mean?

You Can't Take It with You

You can't take it with you, she says,
and I look up from what remains
of my parents' lives—a jumble
of shirts, pants, pocketbooks, shoes—
at Aunt Pat, who shakes her head, sighs,
then tries on a Persian lamb coat, hovers
over a table stacked with silverware, china,
picks up a gravy boat, looking for—what?
a mark? Perhaps, *Limoges?*—then plumps up
the cushions of a silk brocade couch.
Your mother was a pack rat, she says.
How will you ever get rid of this stuff?
I say Rich wants the Chinese breakfront.
I'm taking the Sendai chest.
Once I know what she wants,
a local auctioneer will liquidate the rest.
He'll steal you blind, she says.

A little later I notice the unmistakable scent
of Mom's perfume, try to remember its name,
and Aunt Pat's standing there again,
a long strand of pearls swinging from her neck.
They're mine, she says. *Your mother gave them to me
in 1959. Then, just like her,
she barged into my house and took them back.
That woman caused problems wherever she went.
Your mother was a lulu,* she said.
Then always in a hurry to get I never-
know-where, she doesn't say what else
she wants, or when she'll be back,
just *Remember Chris, money can't buy happiness.*

89

And I stand in the doorway waving her on,
but she doesn't go. She sits in her Mercury Grand Marquis,
then rolls down the window.
What's happening to their Ford Crown Victoria?
And I say, *I don't know.*

What Can You Do?

After Great-Aunt Stella kept feeding the dog
under the table, the Thanksgiving
there was no dog under the table,
Aunt Pat said, *Enough's enough*, and put her
in the nursing home. It was time.
Stella was ninety-two. Living alone. No kids.
Poor thing. That first night, Stella was so befuddled.
She couldn't find the bathroom, piddled on the floor,
slipped, and killed herself.
Of course we were shocked.
But what took us completely by surprise
was the size of Pat's inheritance.
Enough to buy that brand-new Lincoln
she'd had her eyes on. What with all her driving
to bingo and the slots, not to mention
hauling grandkids up and down the interstate,
we all agreed a nice big car made sense.
But when one of the kids let slip
he got to hold the wheel so Pat could fix
herself a highball, cousin Ed flipped.
That's it, Ma, he said. *Leave the car at home.*
Take Amtrak.
Who could blame him?
And then what happened? On the way back
from dropping off the kids in Buffalo—
thank God, they weren't on board—
Pat's train slammed into a freight train
and derailed. They showed footage of the wreckage
on the evening news. From what I hear
Pat was in the dining car drinking a highball.
She got her chest bashed in.
Ed just called from the hospital.
Said he's gonna sue.

Mohegan Sun

Who would've thought he'd live this long?
Aunt Pat said over our breakfast of fruit,
rolls, coffee and eggs, in her complimentary room
on the thirty-first floor, then looked out
the wall of glass to a single hot-air balloon
floating above the river below.

She was talking about Uncle Hubie
whom she never forgave for giving away
his filling station the day they wed—
then *never—not once!*—lifting a finger
to prune, pick, or truck fruit to auction
from the worn-out orchards passed down
from Gram—the farm which at eighty
she'd planned to sell, but which, since Hube's stroke,
she'd mortgaged up to the hilt
rather than hand over *every red cent*
to his nursing home.

Now in the Casino of the Setting Sun
amid the sound of small tinkling bells,
Aunt Pat sits under the bigger-than-life
mechanical wolf, sipping whiskey
and water, relentlessly dropping quarters
into her favorite slot, watching bright colored
cherries, peaches, and apples spin.

Mom's Ring

When the time came, I searched high and low.
Finally, I found Mom's three-carat diamond
set in platinum, surrounded by thirty-two baguettes,
inside a wad of Kleenex at the bottom
of a chipped bud vase, behind a bottle
of Pine-Sol on the top shelf of her broom closet.

Dad bid on the ring at one of those auction houses
along the boardwalk in Atlantic City
after a good night at the craps table.
It came with a certificate of authenticity
claiming Artie Shaw had given it to Fanny Brice
when they got engaged, and Mom had been wanting
to replace her engagement ring—a simple
half-carat solitaire which had been stolen
years before from a hotel room in Acapulco
the winter she was carrying on
with Francisco, a tour bus operator.

It's hard to explain.
But Dad wanted to keep Mom happy,
and since Richard Burton had just bought
Elizabeth Taylor her big diamond,
Mom just had to have it.

Mom was like that.
If her sister, Pat, put in a swimming pool,
she put in a swimming pool. When Aunt Betty
got a hernia, Mom got a hernia.
When Uncle Jack had his heart attack,

she clutched her chest for a month.
And whenever Liz had an affair . . . well!

Funny thing is, even before Mom ballooned
up in weight from all the Prednisone,
she hardly wore the ring.
Now I never wear it. At least not in public.
I can't decide if it looks too grand,
or too gaudy—like something you'd get
out of a gum ball machine.
The man at the jewelry store in town
said he'd pay big bucks for it—more
if I could find those papers—
enough for a trip around the world,
or a new car, which I need.

But I don't know.
Sometimes, on cold, snowy nights,
I like to get a good fire going
in the woodstove, fetch that three-carat diamond
set in platinum, surrounded by thirty-two baguettes,
from where no one will ever find it,
watch it glitter on my finger as I'm turning
the pages of a book.
Mom never read books,
just the *National Enquirer*
to see what Liz was up to.

Web Stalker

Now that I know my first love holds a seat
on the Philippine stock exchange,
flies his own plane, and owns so many
skyscrapers, hotels, shopping malls, and banks
that part of Manila is named after him—
now that I know he has a daughter
the same age as mine, who, like Nicole
was married last year, but according to
The Manila Times On-line,
. . . wearing a Vera Wang gown,
with flowers flown in from Italy . . .
a reception at "Sonrisa," the Ortigases'
summer retreat overlooking the sea,
where many of Manila's top 500
dined alfresco on Mediterranean cuisine . . .
I can't stop thinking of the wealth
I came so close to, so close
that all the rest of my life I'll taste it
whenever I drink Coke from a bottle
or recall the fried pig skins
he and I used to eat at the little kiosk
down the alley from school—
not a kiosk really, more like a lean-to
with a few cases of soda thrown down
on the ground and that cauldron of oil
bubbling over a fire—where he once tipped
Lingoy, the pock-faced young owner
who always wore the same torn pants,
and killed flies with his flip-flops,
an extra peso, then turned to me
and said, *Someday I'll be rich.*

Chapter Six

Blue Socks

When I was sixteen, desperate,
afraid my boyfriend was leaving me,
I spent afternoons sitting in the shade
of a banyan tree knitting him socks,
hoping this act of devotion
would convince him to stay.

Imagine my surprise when one half-
knit cashmere sock showed up
among my father's belongings.
I found it today, inside his flight case,
along with his passport, clip-on sunglasses,
an old picture of me. I don't know what
to make of it, or this sorrow
that never leaves.

Therapy

1.

He always made us tea, using the same
spoon for the sugar and the stirring.
On the low table between us: that lopsided
horse's ass made by an old lady
in ceramics class. He said she said
making it did her more good than his therapy.
A cartridge of razor blades.
One small wooden block. Someone—a boy?—
had whittled ARE YOU CUCKOO
into its side, carved a slot in the top
just the right size to hold his business cards.
My poinsettia. In July I said,
Why don't you just get rid of it?
He said, *Let's see if we can make it bloom again.*

I always think of that room.
The children whose paintings were taped to the walls—
the girl who drew a better Motherwell
than Motherwell, who signed her name
in loopy letters. Everyone—we all had problems.
He kept books on the floor.
Sometimes we looked through the Atlas.
Sometimes he read poems: Bishop, Mirabai,
his own. He said, *Why don't you try?*

I was telling him that in the morning
at the edge of sleep, there might be a second
of silence in my head, then I'd be on
that voyage again, that endless, motionless trip.
The scenes never changed: the island in the Pacific,

the yellow house with the cool stone floor.
That's where he lived, I said. *My first boyfriend.*
I still don't like to say his name.
Paqui. His name was Paqui.
I used to climb the fire escape at school—
go all the way up. If I leaned out far enough,
I could see that patch of yellow, blocks away,
beyond the rooftops.

Then I didn't say any more. I just kept staring
at the threadbare spot in the rug by his feet.
And when I finally glanced up,
I was struck by the look in his eyes: grief . . . mine.

2.

> *When you say, "these things*
> *that come into my mind,"*
> *what do you mean?*

His face. His hands. The bead of sweat
that would sometimes appear on his neck—
I knew just what pore it came out of.
His penis. His voice. Conversations we had.
Places we went. His car. Things like that,
they show up uninvited.

> *How often? Monthly? Weekly?*

How many times did you turn on a light today?

> *How old were you when you met?*

I was thirteen. He was fifteen.

How did you meet?

At a Halloween party. My friend's mother
ran out of candy and he sent his driver
to buy some. That impressed me.

After that how did you get together?

Mostly at the Polo Club, it was a gathering place.
But once he learned how to drive, we spent more
and more time alone. On my sixteenth birthday
we went to a motel. It was my idea.
I was thinking of the Manila Hotel.
It had a verandah and overlooked Subic Bay.
But he said someone might see us
and tell his father. So he drove to a motel
in the red-light district where you could hide
your car in a little garage under your room.
The bed only had a bottom sheet on it.

What happened there?

We undressed, fondled each other.
We didn't have sex. We were saving that
for when we got married. But even though
the place gave us the creeps, after that night
I couldn't imagine not being with him.
I began thinking of ways I could stay
in the Philippines for college, maybe
live at his house on vacations.

How did your parents feel about that?

My Mom——? Who knows? She probably
would've gone along with it. And Dad——

he may have already been transferred
to Okinawa by then, or India. I'm not sure.
It didn't matter though, because
a couple weeks later Paqui changed.
He said I shouldn't have suggested
we go to a hotel. I shouldn't have let him
touch me like that. That now whenever
we were together he had dirty thoughts.
I must've tried to defend myself,
because he shot back, "It's the boy's job to try;
the girl's job to say 'no'." I panicked.
Said we could go to confession. Begged.
But he wouldn't budge. It was over.
Want to hear something funny?
The other night I Googled his wife.
She's the Treasurer of the Family Rosary Crusade.
Anyhow, these things, I try not to let them
into my head, but it's like they live in there—
like he's in my cells. I know it sounds silly
but I really thought we'd be together
for the rest of our lives. I think that's why
divorce has been easy for me.

What do you mean?

Well, besides making bad choices,
I was never really there—in my marriages.
I was off in a foreign country. Each time
I married I hoped it would end
my longing for him. But it never did.
Sometimes I'm convinced I see him in the flesh.

What do you mean?

I'll be somewhere—it happens a lot in airports.
Like last week at the gate, I was sure
he was in front of me. His elbow
gave him away. Sometimes it's his forearm.
Or the back of his neck will glare at me.
I say to myself, "Stop it!
Your mind's playing tricks on you."

      Your mind IS playing tricks on you.

I know that. I just told you.
Can you make it stop?

      Paqui's not the man you long for.

What?

      Your father wasn't there for you.

What?

      Your father wasn't there for you.

Don't say that. It's not true.
My father was there for me. He was.

      Tell me when.

      Tell me when.

3.

Mom was alive again. In the flesh.
Squatting on the back of this couch. Here
by my shoulder. Her eyes, skin, teeth—
they were believable. She popped a handful
of little blue pills into her mouth.
I think it was Equinil. Is Equinil blue?
Maybe it was Thorazine.
Anyway, she was staring down at me.
Next thing, I'm off the couch, crouching
behind you, half-hidden. I'm tugging
at your sleeve, pointing at her, trying
to make you stop scribbling.
Mom's saying, "What did I tell you, Chrissy?
Didn't I say you'd turn out exactly like me?"
Then I woke up.
I can't believe how real that dream was—
really real. Just thinking about it
makes me shake. Why don't we ever talk
about my mother? Whenever I bring her up
you change the subject. Why? You know
my mother was crazy.

I know, Dr. Coursin says with a sigh,
then a wink. *Every session*
when you don't bring her up, I think,
Thank God, I've made it through
another week without having to hear
about her mother. Who in their right mind
would want to talk about that woman?

Divorce

Es verdad, pues reprimamos
esta fiera condición,
esta furia, esta ambición,
por si alguna vez soñamos . . .
  —*Pedro Calderón de la Barca (1600–1681)*

I'm sitting at a little table
by the bakery window
having the mug of tea and raspberry scone
that's my weekly treat after therapy.
If my eyes are swollen it's from
that cry I had after Dr. Coursin said,
There's nothing wrong with you
that wouldn't be soothed by being with a man
who knows how to hold you.
Across the street the UPS man's loading
packages into his truck. I wonder
if he'd know how. Or that bald guy
with the briefcase who just walked by.
No matter how old I get, part of me
stays sixteen, still living in Manila,
still heartsick.
Books help. This bakery's
next to Gibson's Bookstore.
As soon as I finish my snack, I'll check out
the poetry. When Dr. Coursin said,
Why don't you try writing a poem?
I thought he was nuts.
I said, *I don't like poetry.* I forgot
about those words that roll through my head.
Before my boyfriend—that first love

105

you think will never leave you—left,
Srta. Martinez, my Spanish teacher,
taught them to us. I can still see her.
Gray hair. Glasses. The way she stood
beside her desk, ran her finger
down the roster, as one by one she called us
to the front, made us look straight ahead
and recite. She said those words helped her
survive the sight of Japanese soldiers
marching her father off to his death.
I still don't understand them completely—
something about a king, a prisoner,
that we aren't who we are—
I love how they sound, though.
After that boy left I said them over and over.
I'm saying them now.

The Painter

It was spring, chilly, like today.
He was standing on a ladder, leaning
against my upstairs bedroom windowsill.
He was painting the outside trim.
I was painting the inside trim.
Down the road someone was hammering,
whistling a tune I tried to make out,
but the notes kept getting lost in the breeze,
or we'd chat through the screen—the way
strangers do—about the harsh winter,
the endless work of maintaining a house.
I didn't know then that after he closed
that can of green paint, washed his brushes,
and called it a day, the phone would ring,
and I'd be rushing to catch a plane,
dialing the number on his business card,
telling a machine I'd been called away,
where to find the house key—the back lock—
how to jiggle it.
I didn't know I'd sit by Mom's hospital bed
for a month, listening to morphine drip,
adjusting the kink in the long plastic hose
that ran from the hole carved into her throat,
or that sometimes at night as I was bent
over insurance forms, the phone would ring
and it would be him, calling to say
how the job was coming along, asking
if there was any change—was I okay?
Nor did I know that each time since,
whenever he came to paint porches or decks,
as he fell into the honest, simple rhythms

107

of his trade, I'd putter in the garden,
and we'd talk while we worked—
about our comings and goings, the lives
within our lives, a few private griefs, hopes—
or that tonight I'd set out two dinner plates,
my mother's candlesticks, that we'd eat
haddock baked in white wine with vegetables,
then after raising cups of blackberry tea
to that small inn in Maine we hope to own someday,
I didn't know we'd trace the routes
we've each taken to arrive at this moment,
going all the way back to my first kiss,
and the Irish setter pup he won in second grade.

The Wedding

Trying to keep step with the music
and our thin heels from sinking
into the ground, yesterday my daughter
and I walked along the side hill,
past the violinist, past Matty clicking
his camera, past Aunt Pat, Peg, and Tyler
gathered under the shade tree,
past little Helen holding her blankie,
and one hundred others lining the path
to the Japanese maple at the edge
of the pond, and Rob,
the young man Nicole was to wed.
After the few words of better or worse,
a reading from the *Velveteen Rabbit*,
dancing, and a feast: mixed baby greens
with glazed hazelnuts and gorgonzola cheese,
pasta dishes, meat dishes, grilled vegetables,
lobster, and coconut shrimp.
With ten thousand emotions running
through my body, I barely touched my food.
Today, alone again, I stand at the window
stirring my tea. Outside, roses, the small statue
of Buddha, the morning haze. And near the fence,
the open wedding tent, empty now,
except for round tables stripped of their linens,
a few deflated white balloons,
and the lingering voice of one who knows me.
Eat, he says, *Eat*.

Facing the Mirror

Halfway through my favorite step
aerobics class this morning, when Karen,
our instructor called out, *Is everybody glistening?*
instead of my face, red, and dripping sweat,
I saw Gram standing by that old bureau of hers,
shimmying a girdle up the loose flesh
of her thighs, pulling it over her belly,
then, after stopping to catch her breath,
fastening what she used to call *my harness*
around her waist, turning it
till its DDD cups faced ready to catch
her falling breasts. Lucky I didn't trip
and fall—a fear I've had ever since
I began wearing glasses—
and lucky, too, the vision didn't last long,
but it was vivid, so vivid,
that when Karen said, *Ready?*
One more time. Take it from the top!
and I caught myself thinking
about that man I try not to think about—
the one who's so much younger than me—
the one who just yesterday referred to
my daughter's new dog as *your grandpuppy,*
I flew up on my step, and moved
through that routine like a woman possessed.

The Cove

All afternoon we swam from the boat.
Now at the ladder, old Chamois must think
she's a puppy again, trying to climb
into your arms and lick every inch of your face.
The late day sky's turning orange and pink—
almost a music, it makes me want
to take everything in. Mountains. Trees.
That mahogany runabout.
The woman stretched out on the bow reading
a book—or could she be falling asleep?
The young boy fishing off the side.
The other boaters speeding through
the *NO WAKE* zone, waving and shouting,
How do we get to Weirs Beach?
Who could forget them—the look on their faces
when you call back, *Sorry, folks,*
you're on the wrong lake!—?

But what about this dragonfly? It, too,
must be remembered. This swarm of gnats.
That canoe someone abandoned on shore.
The marsh grass growing through its missing bottom.
Its flecked and peeling red paint.
What could be more important than that?
Or what remains of this fish? Its bloated sac
floating in the sun. Its warm, generous scent.
The milky white socket where an eye
used to be.
This moment is already over,
the Buddha once said. *It's changing*
into the next. Moving like the small brown bird

flying past us. Like Chamois, padding around
and around in tight circles, waiting for you
to sit down so she can doze in her favorite
place at your feet. Like the sunlight
flooding your face as you lean forward
to pull up anchor—your eyes: now gold, now amber,
now cinnamon, sunflowers, horses, birds . . .

The Gift

In Japan long ago, when Koson
folded back the sleeves of his kimono,
picked up his pen and began drawing
the image that would later be carved
into cherrywood, then pressed
onto paper and colored in,
he had no idea that a century later
a man in rural New Hampshire
would unpin that print from his bedroom wall
where it had been hanging longer
than he could remember, roll and tie it
with curling red ribbon, then leave his home
in the dark, and drive past frozen fields and woods,
past farmhouses with wreath-covered doors
and candlelit windows, on and on,
to the roadside mailbox of a woman
he hadn't seen in over a year.
He just knew that as he moved that pen,
line by line, feather by feather, beak by beak,
loneliness drew two wild geese flying
before a moon so large it nearly filled
the page.

Chapter Seven

India

Somewhere in the desert, at the bottom
of impossibly steep stone stairs,
inside the underground cell
where he once sat silent
for a year and a half,
the Master tells a story.
A man spent his entire life eating
a car: bumper, headlights, hood—
all of it—piece by piece, bit by bit.
Don't laugh, he says. *Think what it took.*
He then places his thumb on my forehead,
above and between my eyebrows.
Dear daughter, he says, *close your eyes.*
Quiet your mind. Look inside.
And I try. And I try.
But I can't even sit still.

The Road to Rajasthan

You can leave me, but I'll never leave you.
—Ajaib Singh (1926–1997)

Which guru are you here to see?
the Immigration officer asks.

Now outside Customs, our translator, Pappu,
meets us, then leads us through
the airport, noisy with travelers
and those birds that swoop in
from somewhere up by the eaves—
aren't you a cocky little thing, perched
on that Coke bottle pecking at a straw!—
then outdoors, around beggars, bicycles,
rickshaws, mopeds, and taxis, to the lot
where our bus sits ready to take us
on yet another long trip.

What's changed?
Not the smell of incense and diesel fumes.
Not the garland of paper marigolds
and Christmas lights that ring
the inside of the windshield.
Not the picture of that ancient swami—
which one is he—Guru Nanak?—
taped to the rearview mirror.
Not the barefoot young outcast
who sits atop the engine cover
and cleans it, and everything within his reach
with his filthy rag.
And not my thought,
What am I doing here . . . again?

It's evening now. Along the roadside
small fires burn outside shacks
made of cardboard and tin.
They light the faces around them.
Sixteen years ago I came to India
for the first time, sat cross-legged
before Ajaib, closed my eyes, and tried
to glimpse Heaven. Now, who knows
how many attempts later, again I try,
but see my younger self testing him,
How many gurus are there?
That's God's business, he says.

At the dimly lit border crossing,
the guard sits on his rope bed.
Next to him: his turban, a few possessions.
Next to his bed: a cow.
The driver taps the horn.
His helper hops out.
He hands the guard some papers,
and while the groggy guard tackles the job
of getting himself out of bed
and moving the sawhorse that blocks the road,
the boy lifts the hood, wipes the oil stick
on his rag, checks the oil, then climbs
up on the hood, wipes and wipes the bug-
smeared window, and climbs back in.
When the bus moves on, the road is covered
with sand. Outside, barely visible
in the headlights: a sadhu—
you can tell by his saffron colored robes
and the tin cup he waves; an elephant;
two camels: one carrying a man
sitting on a bundle of branches, who turns,
and stares.

It's 3 a.m. At this time tomorrow,
everyone on this bus will be sitting
inside Ajaib's meditation room,
its dirt floor covered with homespun
burlap sacks to keep down the dust.
It's easy to know God, he'll say,
dimming the kerosene lamp,
but first you must know your Self.
That's the hard part.
Now close your eyes.
Still your mind.
Look inside.

I must've dozed off—I'm good at that—
like when I fell asleep and dreamed
I was standing in the courtyard
waiting for old Mustanaji to ladle
the morning chai. *Sorry to wake you,*
Ajaib said, after Pappu shook the little bell,
and, startled, I opened my eyes. *But why*
travel so far to sit at my feet
if all you want is a nap and a cup of tea?

The driver's helper is busy with his rag.
He's wiping our breakfast trays
and polishing apples. A few years ago,
I leaned across the aisle, shook Pappu awake,
and frantically pointed this out to him.
He said something in Hindi.
A moment later the driver's compartment
went dark.
What did you say? I asked.
I said he should unplug the lights so you can't see.

119

At sunrise we approach a small village,
wait, while cows cross the road,
then drive slowly past mud and dung huts,
their doorways decorated with rice paste
drawings of elephants, peacocks,
lotuses and vines. A girl around eight
dips her finger into a bowl, and copies
the lines her veiled mother draws.
I miss my daughter.
I wonder what pictures she and I could paint
on our little house to keep evil away?

—Suddenly, the bus pulls off the road. Shifts gears.
No signposts now. No tracks.
Just sand as far as the eye can see.
How does the driver know where to go?
Six trips and I still can't figure it out.
Can you give me a sign—just a little sign
to show me you're a True Guru? I asked Ajaib.
Satgurus don't perform tricks, he said, speaking
through Pappu. *And even if I did,*
your mind would not give you peace.
How many hours did you meditate today?

Finally, ahead on the left, that canal
built by the British, an irrigated plot,
some leafy trees. It won't be long now.
The driver's helper combs his hair.
A woman in back—I think it's my friend,
Stephanie, starts singing—and the rest of us
join in.

> *Satguru pyare meri, jindagi savar de*
> *Karma de mare tere, dar te pukara de*
> *Tere te guru ji mera, rai rati jor na*
> *Tere bajo dunia te, mera koi hor na*

Closer, you can see a patch of green.
Next to it—hard to make out—a wall,
the color of sand. A door, painted blue.
One afternoon, on the other side
of that wall, when I *wasn't* looking,
I caught a glimpse of Ajaib
sitting off to the side, alone, head bent,
eyes cast down, and I *knew*—
but in a blink, that knowing was gone.
The bus stops beside the wall.
The assistant hops out, places
a plastic step on the ground, and one
by one, we climb down.
Ajaib has come walking from the field,
his palms pressed together in greeting.
Some passengers are crying.
Some are crying and smiling.
The driver's helper just fell—no,
he's dropping to his knees, reaching to touch
Ajaib's feet—Ajaib's dropping faster,
catching hold of the boy's elbow,
lifting him up, gently patting his cheek.
Now he's walking toward me,
looking into my face.
This farmer with the long
white beard, who speaks in Punjabi
of worlds within worlds, and forms
I haven't seen—is he a fake?—
or can he take me to God?

Dear daughter, there are no shortcuts on this path.
Reading and writing are wasted here.
If you want to know who I am, put down
your pen. Put down your pen.

121

What If?

Sitting up to my waist in grass,
watching my godson cast his line
into this familiar lake, I find myself
meditating on my heredity: Joe, my father,
who skipped stones across this water;
Gus, his father, known as Pop,
who built our camp—the little white wooden box
made from three kinds of scrap lumber,
four scrap windows, one scrap door,
and no plumbing, yet a palace
to those of us who waited all winter
to crowd into it. Gone now, they were good
simple people of faith who went to Mass
every Sunday and never spoke ill of anyone.
My younger self. How pious I was at seven.
Dressed in white patent leather, white tulle
and satin, I folded my hands in prayer
and joined the procession to the altar.
Before the painted plaster statue
of Mary with her arms outstretched to me,
and under the large crucifix that hung
suspended from the vaulted ceiling,
I opened my mouth to receive the host,
afraid if I so much as nicked
the thin wafer with the edge of one tooth
it would bleed.
Years later, I wore Birkenstocks, loose cotton
clothing, and made pilgrimages to India.
Waking at three every morning to the sound
of a meditation bell and the smoke
of a burning fire, I sat cross-legged

in the desert, closed my eyes, and tried in vain
to glimpse heaven.
Now, though a few words of Latin and Hindi
remain, I've left the church and guru.
Here at the edge of this lake,
under the blue dome of the sky,
I look at this handsome young boy, so alert
to the little red and white float bobbing
lightly on the skin of the water,
and I can't help wondering, what if
the mystics and saints are mistaken?
What if there is no other side—if all
that exists is this one life. Here. Now. On earth.
What if after my death a fish—say, a trout—
nibbles at particles of my bone and dust
thrown into this lake, grows fat,
then happens to be caught by a child—
if not my godson, perhaps his friend—
the one he builds forts with—who then
carries it dangling from the end of his rod
as he rides his bike up Pond Hill Road,
past the brook and orange daylilies
to the gravel driveway and weathered
rear door of his house? What if
his father takes out a sharp knife and guts it—
if his mother rinses it, pats it dry,
coats it with flour seasoned with salt
and pepper, then melts butter in a large iron skillet,
and when it's foamy, cooks the trout
till the flesh next to the bone is opaque?
What if, along with wedges of lemon
and a few grapes, she arranges the trout
on a warm platter, and after setting
the platter on a pressed linen tablecloth,
joins her husband and son at the table,

and with the evening sun coming through
the screens, together they bow their heads
in a moment of silence?
What if this is what becomes of me after death?
What if this is all? If this is it?
How could I consider myself cheated?
How could I not count myself blessed?

Rhyme

The man sitting next to me on the plane
was tanned. We chatted, laughed
over the pictures in his *Vanity Fair*,
and when he called my attention
to the view he said put his life
into perspective, looked out the window
at the clouds below.
I said that after a year of deaths
and dismantlings, I looked forward
to visiting my daughter, who was studying
in Europe. He spoke of recent vacations,
so many, I teased, *You must not work.*
I'm a lawyer, he said. *Figures*, I said.
But after we handed the flight attendant
our dinner trays, he turned to the side,
unzipped his carry-on, and from a large
white prescription bottle, counted out
a palmful of pills.

What did you say the first time someone
told you they had AIDS?

I sat there dumbstruck, watching him
swallow those pills with water from a clear
plastic cup. But when I heard the concern
in his voice for me: *Is this the first time*
you've met one of us?
I placed my hand on his, and like an old
married couple, we leaned back, and talked
through the night. About my life. His.
The eleven years he'd lived while so many died;

the last few when he, too, was close to death,
and now was not—all because of this new
combination of pills.
Someday, he said, *someday I'll write about it.*
But mostly he talked about the partner he lost.
A psychologist, he said. *He analyzed everything—*
drove me crazy sometimes. But I told him things
I never told anyone before or since.
To him, everything was myth.
He was so smart, he said.
You're smart, I said.
Not like him, he said. *Not like him.*
And then he turned to the window again.

I loved Venice. Each day my daughter
and I drank cappuccino, and ate gelato.
And in every church and cathedral
we entered, I knelt and prayed for the dead.
I wondered where they'd gone.
Then I lit a candle for them,
and one for the man with AIDS.
When we rode the vaporetto, I loved
looking back at the city and the people
strolling beside the canals. I wondered
about their lives. And I wished I was younger.

On the drive through Tuscany, there was mist
in the air. With the *Eyewitness* guidebook
open on her lap, and speaking fake Italian,
Nicole and I laughed ourselves silly
singing the name of each town out loud:
Poggibonsi . . . San Miniato . . .
Bagni de Lucca . . . Torre de Lago . . .
And we squabbled. But not much. Sometimes
at night, when we were tired

and had waited too long to get a room.
And on the Autostrada, because Nicole
was under twenty-five and couldn't drive
the rental, and I let all the cars
sail past us, meaning: I kept it under
a hundred.

I didn't know about Rilke then,
or Keats, or Séverin. Nor did I know
about Eliot, or ever hear April described
as *the cruelest month,*
but after Nicole returned to school,
and I flew home to northern New England,
to the havoc left by winter: the mud,
desiccated leaves, and loneliness—
all the sadness came back. And despair.

So because it was my habit, I wrote
in my journal. If the black flies weren't bad,
and it was warm enough, I sat on my deck
and wrote. If not, I wrote inside, often
into the night. In fact, I did nothing
but write. Mostly about people I'd loved
and lost, places I remembered.
Sometimes I muttered to myself. Sometimes
I stared into space. Sometimes I cried.
And all the while, in the corner
of my eye, the man next to me on the plane
leaned back and listened.
His eyes were blue.
And now I remember—I was writing
about him, and at the same time
I was thinking about Christ on the cross.
And then I was thinking about Lazarus,
how he suffered and died twice.

127

And that's when it happened.
For the first time, the right margin
shattered, some words began to rhyme.

Poetic Medicine: A Conversation

I had a terror—since September—I could tell to none—
and so I sing, as the Boy does by the Burying Ground—
because I am afraid—
        Emily Dickinson (1830–1886)

Sometimes I still wonder
if my mother was crazy
or just acted crazy.

       It can be confusing.

If she'd stayed with one doctor
maybe she could've been helped,
but she hopped around—that's how
she got so many prescriptions.
Then every so often she'd say,
"Dr. So-and-so says I need to get my medicines
straightened out," and she'd pack her negligees
and go into the hospital. When I'd visit,
her nightstand would be covered
with jars of creams and lotions.
If she wasn't tweezing her eyebrows
or painting her fingernails,
she'd be wearing a mud mask,
reading the National Enquirer.
I'd say, "Ma, have you seen the doctor?"
And she'd say, "Which doctor?"
And I'd say, "I don't know. How many ARE there?"
And she'd say, "I don't know."
So I'd say, "Well, do you have a favorite?"
And she'd laugh and say,
"The three I haven't met yet."

I hear you. Caveat emptor.

What does that mean?

> *Buyer beware.*
> *I have a case of it—a lady*
> *in Concord Hospital.*
> *It's hard getting her out of there.*
> *She knows all the angles.*

But when the family would say certain things—
like when Aunt Betty, Mom's oldest sister,
suddenly died, and her sister Pat said to me,
"Why couldn't it have been your mother?"
I'd feel sorry for her. I'd say,
"What if Mom really is sick?"

But sooner or later—who knows why?—
Mom would turn on me, curse,
call me names, make vicious accusations.
And even when I tried to stay present,
I couldn't. I'd float off somewhere,
watch her and think, "You're not sick;
you're mean."

> *What did your father do?*

Nothing. Oh, maybe he'd say,
"Come on, Louise.' But that's it.
I remember once after he and I were alone,
I said, "Dad, do you believe the things
Mom says about me?"
And he said, "Of course not."
So I said, "Then why don't you say so?"
And he said, "Chrissy, what good would it do?"

He was the parent.
It was his job to protect you.
You know that now, right?

I do. And do you know what else I think?
Dad's job—when he'd go overseas alone—
it was his way of floating off like I did.
Sometimes I think it killed him.

What do you mean?

There was so much he blocked out.
Maybe all that forgetting led to
Alzheimer's disease.
After he was diagnosed though,
in her pathetic kind of way
Mom took good care of Dad.
At the end he became one of her fetishes.
She shaved his head, rubbed lotion
on his skin, polished him like a lamp.
Once Dad's doctor asked me,
"What's wrong with your mother?"
I said, "I don't know."
"Well, your parents are in a deep dark hole," he said,
"don't climb in."

What was I supposed to do,
abandon them?

It's over now.

Is it? Look what I did after they died.
When I came back from that trip to Europe,
I acted insane. And when those first poems
broke loose—that poor man I met on the plane—

131

I bet he wishes he never gave me his address.

> *People have done worse.*
> *Besides, you told him you'd stop*
> *sending him your poems if he said to,*
> *and when he said, "Stop,"*
> *you stopped, right?*

And I felt guilty, so that's good.
I don't think Mom ever felt guilt.
But why wouldn't you put me on medication?
When Jonas and I were divorcing you did.
And this was worse.

> *This was different.*
> *Look at what you were doing*
> *with all that grief.*

Did you know that writing poems
would diffuse the memories that haunted me?

> *No. I just know that sometimes*
> *you have to fight fire with fire.*

When I think of that flight—how something
can be right under the surface
and you don't know it—

> *Do you mean your father?*

Yes. Did I already say this?—
when that man told me he was gay
and had AIDS, that he'd been diagnosed
in '86—in SEPTEMBER of '86—I thought,
"That's when Dad was diagnosed."

And then when the plane began to shake
and I clutched his arm—
it's hard to put this into words—I felt death
beneath his skin—and I loved him.
Yet, at the same time, I sensed—
felt through my hand—that some part of him
could never respond to me.
He just wasn't made that way.

Do you think your father was gay?

No. Just distant. Unavailable.
You could feel it in his hugs—
the few he gave—mostly at airports—
when he'd pat me on the back,
and say, "Be good to your mother."
Everyone called me a "trooper" then;
I never cried, never clung.

But you clung to your first boyfriend.

I did. For over thirty years
I saw Paqui's face inside my head.

And then you tried holding on
to a man who was dying.

I did.

Now look at what you're doing.

Keep writing.

How much time do we have left?

A few minutes.

Remember how you said that I have a high-
voltage heart and lots of self-doubt?—
that they battle with each other?
I've been reading Emily Dickinson lately.
She was like that, I think.
And there was someone in her life, a man
whose absence provoked a lot of poems.
   "I live with Him—I see his face—"
That's my favorite.
Emily—she was something—
she put everything into her work.

   Well, stick with her and you'll be okay.

Are we done?

   Not quite.

Do you think I'm getting better?

   Yes.

Does that mean I'll be getting the boot soon?

   You'll never get the boot.
   Someday one of us will die.
   But you'll never get the boot.

If I die first will you come to my funeral?

   Absolutely. I'll be there.

The Bell

Each Sunday for the past twenty years,
I've walked through the woods

to a small satsang hall to hear the words
of wise men, mystics and saints.

God is love, they say, *and the way*
back to God is love.

Each Sunday I sit and listen and watch
the hands of the clock.

At ten minutes until twelve I hear a bell.
It is rung by a man I do not know

who also lives in these woods.
It is said that he tolls the bell

for someone who died long ago,
on a Sunday, at ten minutes until twelve.

Today for the first time in many years,
I did not go to the hall. I stayed home

writing and rewriting the words of this poem.
I lost track of time.

Then I heard the bell.

Epilogue

Again

>>*Hey Christine, are you there? . . .*
>>*Want to come to the courthouse with me?*
That's the e-mail that arrived this morning—
the latest of hundreds that've sailed back
and forth between me and my friend
who lives just on the other side of this hill—
my friend whom I haven't seen in two years
—not since that day on his boat
when my fantasy of becoming his girlfriend
was put to an end.
Think how it feels now to climb into his car—
no longer the blue Jetta that took us places,
and missing old Cham, the gentle Lab
he always boosted up on to the backseat
and brought along—
and when he jokingly points to the receding
hairline I can't see but he swears is there,
and I let out a laugh, and thank God
I just colored my gray, know what memories
this brings up: moments when I'd be done in
by the sight of a woman—half my age?—
pushing a baby in a stroller or grocery cart—
the tangled ache I tried, but could not separate
as I looked through what felt like two pairs
of eyes: his, at what he yearned for,
mine, at what I was too old to give.
And halfway to the courthouse when he tells me
what I've been afraid of: that he's moving—
not to that make-believe Wyoming ranch
I know he carries in his head—but away,
imagine how attached I've been

to knowing he's near: just beyond my woods,
past Abbot's farm, inside his white Cape
overlooking the pond, or woke
to see evidence of this appear on my laptop:
  >>*Good morning, Christine. Go outside*
  >>*right now. Hold a dark colored book*
  >>*at an angle and catch big snowflakes.*
  >>*You will be glad you did.*
But imagine too, how hard I've worked to mean
what I say, *Of course I'm sad, but not too sad.*
And when we stand before the judge,
and that voice inside my head
that likes to float me off to La-La Land,
whispers, *this is almost like getting married,*
know how long it's taken me to get wise to it,
to keep both feet on the ground
beside this man who's stood by me,
who seems a little shaky now
as he finally lets himself shed his name
that's never fit and take the one
he'll turn forty with,
and start a new life with,
and if he gets his wish,
meet the woman he'll share it with—
this name from the list of names
he began years ago,
and I added to,
and we voted on,
and e-mailed back and forth,
and when it came down to three,
then two, then one, tinkered with
the spelling of. And after he signs
the paper that makes it official, puts down
his pen, then opens his arms,
and we hold long and hard, imagine

that day on his boat, when half
out of my mind with fear, and desire,
and grief, I managed to speak
the one clear thought in my head:
I hope you'll be here when I can handle
seeing you again.

C-Section

Today, as I watched my daughter
settle herself and eight-month-old Mia
into their favorite chair to nurse,
I thought back to those first days
after that scary ride to the Emergency,
when Rob and I took turns sleeping
at the hospital, and it was all Nicole could do
to turn from her back to her side
as one of us lifted the baby
(she wasn't named Mia yet)
out of her bassinet, and careful
not to touch Nicole's stomach or press
down on the mattress, helped guide her
to Nicole's breast, then propped her
with a pillow so she wouldn't roll away.
And seeing that room again—the flowers,
the balloons, the well-wishers who gathered
at Nicole's bedside—I remembered Aunt Pat,
who after hearing what had happened,
described what she'd gone through
when her babies were born, saying,
And the first is always the worst!
and the little guy, known to be rambunctious
who said, *I want to be the one to hold the baby!*
I want to be the one to hold the baby!
so we let him but only in the chair
with his father jammed next to him;
and how everyone said, *Oh, isn't she beautiful!*
especially her head, which we all agreed
was perfect—not cone-shaped, or pointy,
or scratched like Nicole's was
when after nineteen hours my doctor said,

Enough's enough, and pulled her out
with forceps. (You can see the claw
marks beside her ears in that first photo
I pasted into her Baby Book.)
And then when Mia finally let go
of Nicole's nipple, stretched her little arms
over her head, and gave her mom
that *Life-doesn't-get-better-than-this* look
that always makes us laugh,
I remembered the morning when the nurse came
and removed Nicole's IV and catheter;
and then the surgeon came
and took her staples out, and one by one
dropped them into a little Ziploc plastic bag
which he gave her as a memento;
and then the nurse came back
and showed her how to take care of the scar;
and then we were alone,
and I don't know what I was doing,
but all of a sudden Nicole, who hadn't panted,
or pressed down, or squatted, or rested,
or pushed and pushed and pushed,
or sweat, or been given ice chips to suck on,
or looked in a mirror and watched
the baby's head crown, or heard Rob say,
Come on Rosebud, give it all you've got!
or felt her emerge, or cried,
cried for one short, hard moment,
then asked, *Mom, can I say I gave birth?*

143

Notes

"Dear Christine" is composed of three letters written by Daniel Nolan in 1957 and found inside a steamer trunk in August 1996.

CavanKerry's Mission

Through publishing and programming, CavanKerry Press connects communities of writers with communities of readers. We publish poetry that reaches from the page to include the reader, by the finest new and established contemporary writers. Our programming brings our books and our poets to people where they live, cultivating new audiences and nourishing established ones.

Other Books in the New Voices Series

Howard Levy, *A Day This Lit*

Karen Chase, *Kazimierz Square*

Peggy Penn, *So Close*

Sondra Gash, *Silk Elegy*

Sherry Fairchok, *Palace of Ashes*

Elizabeth Hutner, *Life with Sam*

Joan Cusack Handler, *GlOrious*

Eloise Bruce, *Rattle*

Celia Bland, *Soft Box*

Catherine Doty, *Momentum*

Georgianna Orsini, *Imperfect Lover*

Christopher Matthews, *Eye Level, 50 Histories*

Joan Seliger Sidney, *Body of Diminishing Motion*

Christian Barter, *The Singers I Prefer*

Laurie Lamon, *The Fork Without Hunger*

Robert Seder, *To the Marrow*

Andrea Carter Brown, *The Disheveled Bed*

Richard Jeffrey Newman, *The Silence of Men*

Ross Gay, *Against Which*

Joseph Legaspi, *Imago*